John Bale

Twayne's English Authors Series

Arthur Kinney, Editor

University of Massachusetts, Amherst

TEAS 520

JOHN BALE FROM *THREE LAWS*, c. 1548
Courtesy of the Bodleian Library, Oxford

John Bale

Peter Happé

Twayne Publishers
An Imprint of Simon & Schuster Macmillan
New York

Prentice Hall International
London • Mexico City • New Delhi • Singapore • Sydney • Toronto

Twayne's English Authors Series No. 520

John Bale
Peter Happé

Twayne Publishers
An Imprint of Simon & Schuster Macmillan
1633 Broadway
New York, New York 10019

Library of Congress Cataloging-in-Publication Data

Happé, Peter.
    John Bale / by Peter Happé
        p.   cm.—(Twayne's English authors series)
    Includes bibliographical references and index.
    ISBN 0-8057-7048-8 (cloth)
    1. Bale, John, 1495–1563—Criticism and interpretation.   2. Bale, John,
1495–1563—Dramatic works.   3. Reformation—England.
I. Title.   II. Series.
PR2209.B2H27   1996
828'.209—dc20   96–10767
                                                                                                            CIP

The paper used in this publication meets the minimum requirements of American
National Standard for Information Sciences—Permanence of Paper for Printed Library
Materials. ANSI Z39.48–1984. ∞™

10 9 8 7 6 5 4 3 2 1

Printed in the United States of America

Contents

v

Editor's Note

John Bale partly inherited and partly created the cultural and historical traditions that led in time directly to the work of Spenser, Shakespeare, and other later Renaissance poets and dramatists. Here Peter Happé, the distinguished editor of *The Complete Plays of John Bale*, shows just what this legacy was. Both as a Catholic in the Carmelite order and then as an outspoken Protestant polemicist, Bale produced works of great power that managed to combine ardent religious belief, historical occurrence and consequence, and dramatic effectiveness. By examining all the extant manuscripts and the various states of Bale's published works, Happé for the first time gives a definitive analysis and evaluation of one of the most prominent and influential voices of the English Reformation. What emerges is a portrait of a man of deep convictions, literary ingenuity, and poetic experimentation. In addition to reviewing Bale's body of work, Happé shows in considerable detail how Bale's plays were probably staged, adding important knowledge to our present understanding of the morality play, the interlude, and Tudor theatrical performance. This accessible yet deeply learned study will be mined for years to come by scholars and students alike in religion, history, drama, and theater history of the English Renaissance and Reformation.

Arthur F. Kinney

Preface

In writing this book I have attempted to bring together information and opinions about the life and works of John Bale as a whole. To do this means to survey what he would no doubt have regarded as the heart of his life—his religious belief, deeply held when he was a Catholic and even more passionately proclaimed once he accepted the new Protestant ways. With his convictions at the center, one can try to integrate his extensive work as a dramatist—he claims to have written more than 20 plays—with his lifelong habit of collecting information about books from the past, and with his construction of a polemical view of history, giving special reference to the English Church. The narrative of his life, the subject of chapter 1, draws attention to the psychological and sometimes physical hardships which were typical of the lot of many people in an age of political and religious turmoil. It was a form of existence in which persecution played a large part, and one in which it was sometimes necessary to defend oneself vehemently.

To carry out this task I have looked at the four printed plays which are extant, as well as at *King Johan* which survives in a uniquely interesting manuscript now in the Huntington Library. Apart from the bibliographical and religious interest of these works, they are remarkable for the dramatic skills which they embody. Although there is a strong likelihood that they were performed in Bale's lifetime, it appears that they have rarely been done since, and it has therefore seemed important to offer an account of their dramatic qualities and their theatrical possibilities. Such an account inevitably depends upon somewhat subjective analysis and interpretation, but it has been possible to identify certain features of staging embedded in the text supporting the view, which can also be externally sustained, that Bale was an experienced playwright and knew what he was about. The time when he was most active in the drama, the fourth decade of the 16th century, was one of importance in the development of the English theater, as the work of John Heywood and John Redford suggests. It was also one in which the long-established Corpus Christi plays and cycles were still being actively promoted in many English towns and cities. My consideration of these aspects will be found in chapters 4, 5, and 6, which discuss the individual plays, supported by a separate treatment of staging in chapter 7. Finally, chapter 8 suggests that, whether influence can be proved or not, Bale's plays form a part of the increasingly resonant drama of Protestant England, which grew in strength as the century progressed.

Bale was studious by nature throughout his life. On the one hand, this led to his intensive study of what we would now term the history of literature, even though the present-day concept of "literature" is hardly sustainable in the 16th century, and Tudor "history" is not quite the same as the modern academic discipline. His work in this field was intrinsically purposeful and largely patriotic. He wanted to preserve a literary inheritance that he, and others, felt was in danger of disappearing; and he also wanted to show a divine intervention in human history which bore down especially on his own troubled times. In dealing with the political and religious history of the period, I have relied extensively upon books by A. G. Dickens, Christopher Haigh, and J. J. Scarisbrick, which are cited in the Selected Bibliography.

A good deal of Bale's work remains in his manuscript collections, which will probably never be published. Some of these deal with historical and mythical aspects of the Carmelite order to which he belonged for the first half of his life. The culmination of his work as a collector, however, was the publication of his two monumental catalogs of "British" writers, together with extensive accounts of their lives and works, in the *Summarium* (1547) and the *Catalogus* (1557–58). As these works are in Latin throughout, I have tried to give an account of them in chapter 3.

On the other hand, Bale's scholarship, especially his work on the Bible, could be pressed to more specifically controversial use. He thus took a vigorous part in written debate. Although there is some truth in the view that he was often too outspoken in his polemics, it was still the work of his convictions, and he would have felt compelled to use his learning in support. Some account of his controversial work will be found in chapter 2, as the study of it seems to me to be a useful approach to detailed consideration of the objectives in the plays.

It is in these works of controversy and in the plays that I should like to suggest that Bale's strongest verbal skills may be found, and I have made a particular point of investigating and discussing these throughout this study. At times, and despite what has commonly been attributed to him, he speaks clearly and engagingly, whether in his own voice or through the words of his dramatic characters, such as King Johan. Based initially, it would seem, upon the language of his native Suffolk, his expression often shows the force and vigor of spoken English, rich in proverbs and sharp in turns of phrase. In addition, there are traces of an interest in poetic expression which shows itself most notably in the often satirical force of his dramatic characters. I have tried to show that Bale's extensive use of English verse was discriminating and effective.

I should like to acknowledge the help I have received from a number of other students of John Bale in writing this book. I learned much during my collaboration with John N. King on our edition of the *Vocation*. Works by William T. Davies, Jesse W. Harris, Honor C. McCusker, and Leslie P. Fairfield, cited in the Selected Bibliography, have been of infinite value to me over a number of years and remain essential to all scholars of Bale; and I have greatly enjoyed John Arden's novel, *Books of Bale*, which he kindly sent me some years ago.

Chronology

1535   Thomas More is beheaded.

1536   Bale is examined by Archbishop Lee of York. Bale leaves Carmelites and becomes a stipendiary priest at Thorndon, Suffolk. Bale is attacked for preaching against Aquinas and against ceremonies.

1537   Complaint against Bale's preaching, on 7 January. Bale is imprisoned at Greenwich by 25 January. John Leland's letter to Thomas Cromwell in support of Bale.

Bale's *Answer to Certain Articles*. Bale is rescued by Thomas Cromwell. Bale is married to Dorothy.

1538   Bale's *King Johan* is written or revised. Payment by Cromwell for Bale's play at Canterbury, on 8 September. Bale writes *Three Laws* (perhaps earlier), *John Baptist*, *Temptation*, and *God's Promises*. Bale writes *Anglorum Heliades*, for John Leland.

1539   Payment by Cromwell for Bale's play about King Johan. Six Articles.

1540   Fall of Cromwell: Bale, Dorothy, and family flee to (?) Antwerp.

1542   Bale's books are forbidden by royal proclamation.

1543   *Customable Swearers*, Antwerp. *A Man of Sin*, Antwerp. MS translation of *William Thorpe*.

1544   *Epistle Exhortatory*, *John Oldcastle*, Antwerp.

1545   Dorothy Bale goes to Norwich on 25 June. *The Image of Both Churches*, *A Mystery of Iniquity*, Antwerp. *Pammachius* (probably not Bale's translation) is performed at Christ's College, Cambridge.

1546   Accusations against possessors of Bale's books in London. *The Acts of English Votaries*, Antwerp. Bale moves to Wesel. *First Anne Askew*, *Rhithmi*, Wesel.

1547   *Latter Anne Askew*, *God's Promises*, *Temptation*, [*John Baptist*], Wesel.

1548   *Summarium*, *Three Laws*, Wesel. Bale edits *Godly Meditation*, and John Lambert's *Treatise*, Wesel. *Answer to a Papistical Exhortation*, Antwerp. Bale returns to England. *Christian Exhortation*.

1549   Bale edits John Leland's *Laborious Journey*. *Dialogue. . .Two Children*.

1550   *Rank Papist*.

1551   26 June Bale becomes Rector at Bishopstoke Hampshire. Performance of *Three Laws* is prepared.

1552   Bale is appointed Bishop of Ossory on 15 August. *Expostulation*.

1553   Bale departs for Ireland on 21 January. Performances of *God's Promises*, *John Baptist*, and *Temptation* at Kilkenny on 20 August. Bale departs from Ireland in September; escapes to Wesel. *Vocation*, Wesel. Bale translates Gardiner's *De Vera Obedientia*.

1554   Dispute among English exiles at Frankfurt. *Dialogue. . . Two Neighbours*. John Foxe, *Commentarii*.

1556   At Basel with Foxe; enrolled at university.

1557   *Catalogus*, Basel.

1558   *Acta Romanorum Pontificum*, Basel.

1559   *Catalogus* additions, Basel. Bale returns to England; Elizabeth I writes to St. Leger about Bale's books.

1560   Bale becomes canon at Canterbury on 10 February. On 30 July Bale writes letter to Matthew Parker.

1561   *Declaration*.

1563   Bale dies on 15 November. Foxe, *Acts and Monuments*.

1574   John Studley translates *Acta Romanorum Pontificum* as *The Pageant of Popes*.

Note on the Illustrations

Bale's printed works contain a large number of woodcuts. It is to be regretted that their full extent, variety, and quality have never been adequately reviewed or catalogued. They are often provided to give the reader a visual edge on Bale's polemical purpose, but their aesthetic quality should also be appreciated. For example, the *Summarium* contains a portrayal of Bale presenting his book to the young King Edward VI, and the *Godly Meditation* shows Princess Elizabeth, book in hand, kneeling at the feet of Christ.

Many of the illustrations are tiny, decorated capitals. In *Votaries* the letter F shows monks reading in a scriptorium, the letter I, a bearded man instructing a woman. *Image*, the commentary on the book of Revelation, includes perhaps the most sustained sequence based upon its highly dramatic symbolism. Two are illustrated here. Figure 1 (p. 47) is the Son of Man: "And he had in his right hand seven stars: and out of his mouth went a sharp two-edged sword: and his countenance was as the sun shineth in his strength. And when I saw him I fell at his feet as dead" (Revelation 1:16–17). Figure 2 (p. 48) shows the binding of Satan: "And I saw an angel come down from heaven, having the key of the bottomless pit and a great chain in his hand. And he laid hold on the dragon, that old serpent, which is the Devil, and Satan, and bound him a thousand years" (Revelation 20:1–2). Illustrations in the two parts of *Anne Askew* of her martyrdom for her bible-based faith include a woodcut of an angel holding a "Biblia" and trampling upon a dragon who wears a triple (papal) crown.

In this volume figure 3 (p. 49), from *Vocation*, illustrates the complex of emotions about persecution Bale experienced during his time in Ireland; and the remarkably beautiful title page to *Three Laws* (figure 4, p. 72) shows, in a multifaceted design, the creation of Eve (left), Eve taking the apple (top), the expulsion (right), and the labors of mankind blessed with children (below).

There are two portraits of Bale in his printed works—one in *Three Laws* (see frontispiece), the other, a portrayal of a much older Bale, in the *Catalogus*.

The frontispiece and figure four are reprinted by permission of the Bodleian Library from *Three Laws* (Malone 502). Figures one, two, and three are reprinted by permission of the Syndics of Cambridge University Library from *The Image of Both Churches* (Hib.8.54.4), and from *The Vocation of John Bale* (Hib. 8.55.1).

Chapter One
Life

Before Conversion

John Bale had a long and productive life. He was born at Cove in Suffolk on 21 November 1495 at a time when England was still a medieval society, and a fairly insignificant country on the edge of Europe. By the time of his death in 1563, the medieval world had been comprehensively transformed, and after a period of agonizing change England was on the verge of a massive expansion, about to emerge as one of the leading nations of Europe. Central to this change was the revolution in religion whereby the ostensibly conforming Church, deeply pious by the standards of Roman Catholicism, was turned into a Protestant institution jealously guarding its religious independence, and guaranteed by the monarchy. The process whereby this came about was a tortuous one, and to have survived through such challenging times was quite a feat in itself; for Bale it was more than this, since he was able to contribute in many different ways to the changes which took place. At times he was the initiator of new ideas and concepts which promoted change; at other times he was more of a victim of forces set in motion by others.[1]

As will be seen from the following narrative, a great deal is known about Bale's life, not least because four of his own accounts of it have survived. These are:

Bodleian *MS Selden Supra 41*, fol. 195 (revisions c. 1536–9)
Anglorum Heliades in British Library *Harley MS 3838*, fols. 111v–112v
Summarium, 242–6
Catalogus, 702–5.

In addition, he wrote and published a detailed narrative in the *Vocation*, describing his appointment to the bishopric of Ossory in Ireland and his adventurous escape from there in 1553. The writing of these accounts forms part of a wider nexus relating to his religious experience and to his own concept of his role as a writer and preacher. Nevertheless, it is to be expected that we shall find some points in his life when it is not at all clear exactly what happened. This is partly because the concept of himself that he attempts to construct is determined by the very forces

1

referred to here. Moreover, the hindsights embodied in his writings may not be strictly related to events as they actually occurred years before. These hindsights may be part of a deliberate process of reconstructing the past to fit with later polemical needs, but they may, alternatively, be due to lapses in memory.

In the *Catalogus* (1557 and 1559), the fullest account of his life, he declares that the poverty of his parents, Henry and Margaret Bale, and their large number of children led them to send him into the Carmelite order at the friary in Norwich. Bale's account is written from his later Protestant point of view; he does not hesitate to vilify what he had come to see as the shortcomings of his upbringing, which he describes as "the abyss of the Carmelite order," his parents being "deluded by the tricks of pseudo-prophets." He says that he entered the friary at the age of 12, and many years later he recalled seeing while he was still a child the burning of Thomas Norrice, the heretic "for havyng the lordes prayer in English." While this may have been traumatic, we should also bear in mind that his later references to the event were related to his polemical purposes. Similarly, he later made much of the sexual excesses of the members of the order; but it is not clear that he was ever a victim of these, however vilely he regarded them.

As far as we can tell, he followed an orthodox curriculum which eventually led him to Cambridge in 1514. He probably entered Jesus College, a relatively recent foundation which at this time was quite small. Among those he would have met there was Thomas Cranmer, a fellow of the college.[2] Bale also speaks of studying in the Faculty of Philosophy with Robert Barnes, the Augustinian, as a fellow student.

Bale remained at Cambridge on and off until about 1529, when he was admitted to the degree of bachelor of divinity (B.D.). His earliest surviving autograph manuscripts date from this period, showing that he was concerned with the instruction of the young, and also with the accumulation of devotional writings and historical material which supported his Catholic beliefs and in particular preserved details of the history and practices of the Carmelites. His work in this period is entirely orthodox, showing special devotion to the Virgin. Nevertheless, it has some individual features which may be an index to his temperament. On the one hand, he is expressly concerned with devotional procedures in the form of hymns and prayers, and on the other, he shows very little interest in the propositions and arguments of traditional theology. At this stage in his work the argument and discourse of patristic writers do not seem to have interested him very much. He looked rather toward chronicling the

events of the history of his order, recording the names of its principal figures, and detailing some of their achievements. Already in his work there
are clear signs of meticulous recording and deliberate and systematic
accumulation of detail. It will be seen in his later work that he had much
to do to develop a methodology, and in this respect his achievement was
to become pioneering.

During this time he no doubt progressed through the usual stages of
professional training. There is no record of his attaining B.A. or M.A.
degrees, although he must have passed through these on his way to the
B.D. already mentioned. By 1534 he was using the title Doctor of
Divinity (D.D.),[3] and if this distinction was achieved by progressing
through the usual curriculum, he would have reached it some 18 years
after entering Cambridge. He was made deacon in 1516, and by 1520
he seems to have been instructing younger novices in his order.

There is evidence that he made at least two journeys abroad at this
time. In 1522 or 1523 he visited Carmelite houses in the Low Countries,
compiling during the journey most of the important notebooks known
as *MS Bodley 73*, which he called *Collectiones Germanicae*, and *MS Selden
Supra 41* (both now in the Bodleian Library) on the history of the order.
In 1527 he made a much longer journey to France, traveling as far south
as Toulouse; the results of this are to be found in another notebook,
British Library *MS Harley 1819* (probably to be identified as the
Collectiones Gallicae). Near Toulouse he stayed with the Carmelite
William Gregory. At this time he rejected an invitation for a prolonged
stay.[4] On these journeys he may well have come into contact with
Continental religious drama, still largely Catholic in orientation. We also
find him writing a Latin antiphon to the Virgin at Hitchin in 1526. The
first line reads:

Hail flowering blossom of Carmel, the Father's pious daughter!
(*MS Harley 1819*, fol. 87v; trans. L.P. Fairfield)

The lost works, *Spirituale Bellum* and *Castellum Pacis*, seem to have been
on traditional subjects for poetry or drama. Not only are the later plays
all in verse, but also there is evidence that Bale continued to be interested in it and to write it. At one point in his account of his writings he
refers to his songs (*carmina*).

While Bale was involved in these eminently orthodox activities, the
first stages of the Reformation were unfolding. It is remarkable that we
know little of his reaction to the early changes, and that the later auto-

biographical accounts do not suggest that Bale was in the least interested in Martin Luther's publication of his *Ninety-five Theses* in 1517, nor in Luther's revolutionary *Address to the Christian Nobility*, *Babylonish Captivity*, and *Freedom of a Christian*, all of which appeared in 1520. Later in life Bale was very much aware of the contents of these works, and we shall see that his plays and polemical prose show a close affinity with many of the items of Luther's arguments at this time. Luther meanwhile drew a response from Henry VIII which earned the king the papal title of Fidei Defensor in 1521. At Cambridge a radical group which included Thomas Cranmer were meeting at the White Horse tavern to debate new issues from about 1520, but there is no positive evidence to show that Bale took any interest in what was going on there. In the *Catalogus* he says: "at Cambridge I wandered in complete barbarism of scholarship and blindness of mind . . . until with the word of God shining forth the churches began to be recalled to the purest springs of true theology" (701). Besides Cranmer and Barnes, future reformers who were Bale's contemporaries at Cambridge included John Barret, Thomas Bilney, John Lambert, Miles Coverdale, Hugh Latimer, Matthew Parker, and William Tyndale. Bale certainly came to respect and acknowledge these men later in life, but in view of his remark above, it seems probable that he derived nothing from them in his youth.

Conversion

It is not until after 1530 that signs begin to appear that Bale was actually turning away from the traditional doctrines. We can identify certain events which suggest that he was moving toward a Protestant viewpoint, but it is very hard to say precisely when there was a definite break. Perhaps indeed it is vain to try to pinpoint the change, because it is conceivable, if not probable, that many small changes of belief and outlook had to take place before a comprehensive Protestant belief could be acknowledged. Some such signs might be inward, reflecting thought and belief internally; others would be more public. In a period when both Catholics and Protestants could suddenly find themselves in mortal danger over their beliefs, the way toward change could not have been easy, especially as great political imperatives could overshadow religious belief from time to time.

The beginning of the decade of the 1530s found Bale still apparently in an orthodox position. He took up an appointment as prior at Maldon by 1530, and about two or three years later he moved to a similar posi-

tion at Ipswich. It was probably at this time that he came into contact
with Thomas, Lord Wentworth, of Nettlestead near Ipswich. Wentworth
was a prominent courtier, cousin of Queen Jane Seymour and Protector
Somerset, and a patron of Protestants. Bale a few years later acknowledged that Wentworth played a significant part in his conversion.

During the same decade, we may suppose that Bale began to take an
interest in writing plays. There are some external factors which might
have encouraged this. He had been brought up in East Anglia which, it
is apparent, had a very strong and diverse dramatic culture. There are a
number of centers including Bury St. Edmunds, Chelmsford, Norwich,
and Cambridge, where drama of many different kinds is known to have
taken place before and during Bale's time.[5] At Ipswich the Carmelites
themselves had taken a significant interest in the Corpus Christi plays.

The positive evidence of his growing personal interest comes from his
lists of his own plays in the autobiographies. The most significant comparison of these is that between his *Anglorum Heliades*, which he wrote
for Leland about 1536, and that in the *Summarium* of 1548. The earlier
account states that he wrote comedies and tragedies in English for John
Vere, the fifteenth (but first Protestant) Earl of Oxford. The *Summarium*
list is longer than the first and shows that he had written more plays on
subjects in common with the Corpus Christi cycles. The following list of
(translated) titles combines the lists in *Anglorum Heliades* and in the
Summarium:

1. Life of Saint John the Baptist
2. Christ and the Twelve
3. *Baptism and Temptation
4. *The Raising of Lazarus
5. *The Council of the Priests
6. *The Meal at the House of Simon the Leper
7. *The Supper and the Washing of the Feet
8. The Passion of Christ
9. Burial and Resurrection
10. †On the Lord's Prayer
11. †The Seven Deadly Sins
12. On the King's Two Marriages
13. Papist Sects
14. Against Fools and Critics
15. Betrayals of the Papists
16. Against Pervertors of the Word
17. *King Johan*

18. The Betrayal by Thomas Becket
19. *God's Promises*
20. *John's Preaching*
21. *The Temptation of Our Lord*
22. *Three Laws*
23. *The Image of Love
24. *Translation of the Tragedy of Pammachius

All these are lost except for those italicized. Titles marked with an aster-
isk (*) are not in *Anglorum Heliades* and may be later than 1536; those
with a dagger (†) are not in the *Summarium*.

The work on the three biblical plays which survive was apparently
designed to recreate the traditional cyclic drama from a Protestant viewpoint. But it is striking that two plays (and only two), one called *On the
Lord's Prayer* and another called *The Seven Deadly Sins*, are omitted from
the later list. Both these subjects could conceivably have been written in
a traditional mode influenced by the medieval genres of the *Pater Noster*
and the morality plays. Of course it is possible that, like the extant plays,
these were written to subvert the traditional modes and themes.
However, their omission from the later list suggests that Bale had come
to disown them. It looks as though he was also writing on subjects of
immediate contemporary and perhaps political interest: plays called *On
the King's Two Marriages*, *The Betrayal by Thomas Becket*, *Against Pervertors of
the Word*, *Papist Sects*, and *Betrayals of the Papists* are to be found on the lists.

Public events at this time may well have played a part in the changes
in Bale's outlook. Between 1530 and May 1532 the resistance of the
English clergy to the king's authority collapsed. Charged under the
Statute of Praemunire, the clergy submitted to Henry by the latter date.
In 1532 Cranmer became Archbishop of Canterbury, and in 1533 the Act
in Restraint of Appeals limited the right of the Church to appeal to Rome
in defiance of royal authority. Cromwell became the king's secretary in
1534, the year that saw the Act of Supremacy establish royal authority
over the Church of England. At about this time Bale moved to Doncaster
to become prior of the Carmelites, and there is every likelihood that the
pressure of these public events encouraged his changing opinions. It is
notable that the Protestant concept of the power of the monarch over the
religious life of the country was one to which Bale came to give enduring
support. It is a leading theme of *King Johan* which, as we shall see, was
probably in existence in some form by now. Doncaster was a city which
had a considerable dramatic heritage, and it may well be that Bale

entered further into the writing of biblical plays in his new environment.[6] He was licensed to preach at York on 24 July 1534, and became embroiled in mutual abuse with a conservative Franciscan called Thomas Kirkby.[7] A commission was set up by Archbishop Edward Lee of York to inquire into the matter. In 1536 Bale was examined again by the archbishop over some articles of belief, one of which was the issue of "honorynge and prayenge to the sayntes." Whatever the dating of the plays, it is clear that by now Bale was taking a stance over some issues of doctrine. Possibly Bale was still at this point interested in reform from within the Church and within the Carmelite order. If so, the next few years saw a significant change in his expectations.

Whether or not the encounter with Archbishop Lee was decisive, Bale moved to London in 1536, and it is at this point he apparently left the Carmelites. He took with him a great deal of knowledge of the history of this order, and, by inference, of other orders too; and one might also recognize that his time in the order—he had been a member since 1508—shows a capacity for religious commitment which he now switched, with the ferocity of a zealot, to the Protestant cause. In both the *Summarium* and the *Catalogus* he speaks of the Church returning to the springs of true theology, and in the *Catalogus* he adds,

> *ab arido monte in floridam ac foecundam Evangelii vallem transferebar.*
> (I was carried by divine goodness from the arid mountain to the flowery and fruitful valley of the Gospel. [702])

This is an idealized figure poetically expressed which reflects how he thought of his conversion more than 20 years afterward.

Although we can identify a number of events in Bale's life in this busy decade it remains difficult to be sure of the precise order in which they happened. On returning to the south, Bale, no longer a friar, probably sought patronage. He must have met John Leland, the King's Antiquary by this time, and begun to work for him, writing a conservative history of the Carmelites, the *Anglorum Heliades*. This work includes a dedicatory letter written at Ipswich in 1536, and it contains material up to about 1539. One section contains a catalog of Carmelite writers (fols. 156–256), and there are two chapters on the deterioration of the Carmelite order in recent times. Perhaps this work is pivotal in Bale's developing a critical attitude to an order to which he had been deeply attached. Here Bale advanced further along the route of biography and bibliography in anticipation of the *Summarium*. As this is also the time of the first phase in the dissolution of the monasteries, it is likely that in working with Leland he came to share an awareness of the danger to monastic libraries which now arose. Bale claims to have spent three years working in Carmelite and Augustinian libraries at this time.

His next move was to make a more certain step toward securing a livelihood by accepting the living of the parish of Thorndon in Suffolk, once more coming into the sphere of influence of Wentworth. However, Bale quickly antagonized the more conservative elements in the locality. A complaint was made about his preaching on the Ten Articles and on Thomas Cromwell's Injunctions, and Bale was imprisoned at Greenwich on the order of Stokesley, Bishop of London. The content of Bale's preaching was attacked in a series of articles which embodied the views of the local conservatives. Bale, from the discomfort of prison, wrote his *Answer to Certain Articles*, which gives an insight into his views at the time, though the items he deals with are determined primarily by what was alleged rather than being a deliberate credo.[8] His reply questions the validity of honoring the saints and also questioned the doctrine of purgatory. He puts great emphasis upon the primacy of scripture over ceremonies, and he deprecates Latin prayers. He gives one hint about his writing of plays containing traditional doctrine: apparently he had shown Christ fighting with the devils in a play called *Harrowing of Hell*. The *Answer to Certain Articles*, extant as a holograph, is one of the first of his writings to give direct evidence of Bale's new thinking. It can be dated January 1537. The plays which have survived cannot be pinpointed quite so accurately, even though we may suspect that some of them were written before his imprisonment at Greenwich. It says a good deal about the political climate at the time that this overtly Protestant document did not result in further difficulties for Bale. It must have appealed to someone in authority.

In the *Catalogus* Bale claims that Cromwell secured his release on account of the comedies he had written. Bale actually says *semper* (always), suggesting that Cromwell helped him more than once. Certainly there is extant a letter from the imprisoned Bale to Cromwell,[9] and we shall see that there is independent evidence that Cromwell subsequently did support Bale the dramatist with money. In addition, there is no doubt that John Leland intervened on Bale's behalf by writing to Cromwell on 25 January 1537.

Bale gives a scriptural reason for marrying at this time. It is unlikely that he was married when at Thorndon, as there would in all probability have been a conservative objection if he had. In reaction against the celibacy of priests in the Roman Church, he was able to invoke the guidance of St. Paul: better to marry than to burn (*Summarium*, fol. 243). In doing so Bale asserts that he was exercising Christian liberty, a phrase reminiscent of Luther. His wife Dorothy remains a shadowy figure. She probably already had at least one son when they married, for she traveled from exile to Norwich to secure the son's apprenticeship in 1545.[10] At that time she was, according to Bale, imprisoned and examined. Four years later Bale published in London *A Dialogue or Communication to be had at a table between Two Children gathered out of the holy scriptures by John Bale for his two young sons John and Paul* (John is the elder). It is not clear whether one or both of these sons were Bale's own children or were Dorothy's children from a previous marriage. Dorothy went with Bale to Ireland and into his second exile in 1553, although Bale does not mention the children at that point. A son called John turns up later, during a dispute at Canterbury in 1560 (although it is as well to remember that families often used the same Christian name for more than one child).

The years 1537–40 are likely to have been the ones during which Bale was most active as playwright and performer. As we have seen, he wrote a large number of plays in the 1530s. The three which survive as incunabula were all printed in 1547–48 in Wesel, together with *The Temptation*, which is extant in an eighteenth-century copy printed from the Wesel original. All give 1538 as the date of "compilation," which suggests that this was the year which Bale regarded as the most significant.

The support he mentions from Cromwell, however, must have come somewhat earlier if it was to affect his hopes of release from prison in 1537. It is notable that the phrase Bale used in the *Catalogus*—*ob editas comedias*—("on account of comedies written" [702])—seems to refer to writing rather than performing. The case of *King Johan*, which was not printed as far as we know, is more complex. It is mentioned in all the lists of plays. The existing manuscript was originally copied by an unknown scribe. Bale made extensive corrections, some of them as late as the first years of Elizabeth I's reign. Equally important, however, there are external references to the play which suggest that it was in existence in some form at least as early as 1536. Because of the composite nature of the manuscript, it is impossible to give the play a single date of composition, or indeed to be certain what form it actually took at any given time. Parts can be dated, such as the reference to the burning of Darvell Gathyron (l.1229) which is known to have happened on 30 May 1538, and which occurs in the continuous manuscript in the scribe's hand.[11]

Some light may be shown on this by the possibility that Bale also took part in the performing of his plays during these years. All four printed plays list him as the Prolocutor, a role which is clearly of theatrical as well as of doctrinal importance. In the case of *Three Laws* there is a doubling scheme in the printed copy. The Prolocutor is doubled with the Vice, Infidelity—the largest and most prominent role. The payment made by Cromwell to "Balle and his fellowes" in September 1538, and again early in 1539 suggest that Bale was the leader of the troupe.[12] Cromwell became Lord Privy Seal in July 1536, and references to payments to the Lord Privy Seal's Players at Thetford in 1537–38, and to the Lord Cromwell's Players at Cambridge in 1537–38 and 1539–40 may also allow the supposition that for a while at least Bale and his players were on the road as part of Cromwell's propaganda effort in the critical years following the Pilgrimage of Grace in 1536.[13] Foxe notes that Cromwell encouraged ballads and books concerning the suppression of the Pope.[14] In *King Johan* the response to the threat from the Catholic alliance, and the prominence of the satire on auricular confession, may be the result of political exigencies.[15] Bale does not mention anything in the autobiographies which gives any support to the possibility of his active role, but in these later accounts the image of his appearing as a traveling player may not have accorded with other more respectable or more theological aspirations. No evidence has emerged that Bale returned to Thorndon after the episode at Greenwich. There is no doubt that the plays as we have them give very strong internal support for the theory that they are manifestly theatrical documents bearing evidence of performance. As we shall see, the scribe who copied the first earlier text of *King Johan* had some difficulty in fitting in the stage directions.

First Exile

Apart from the unpublished notebooks containing information about the Carmelite order, the works written by Bale before 1540 which are known to us consist almost entirely of the plays, and even these were published later than 1540. From them we can derive some salient features of Bale's Protestant beliefs. These place him in a position close to that of Cromwell. He attacks the celibacy of the clergy as hiding corrupt sexual morality, and he brings pressure to bear upon auricular confession in the character of Sedition in *King Johan*, a process which derives from Bale's strong support for royal supremacy. It has been noted that Bale's strongly political objections to this practice do not seem to have been based upon a criticism of the sacrament of penance, as might have been expected.[16] He also attacks the worship of the saints, and encourages the use of the Bible in English as the central part of the Christian experience. Cromwell's administrative measures gave strength to many of these items, but as the 1530s drew to a close, a conservative reaction was supported more and more by King Henry. He wanted the English Church to be independent of Rome, as it now was, but also wanted it to remain Catholic in spirit. As early as 1530 Henry had boasted to the papal Nuncio that, as head of the Church, he would suppress the Lutherans.[17] Cromwell's fall in 1540 was the result of a political maneuver against Henry, but it was also recognized as a disaster to the Protestant supporters, not least because Robert Barnes, whom Bale notes had been much influenced by Luther, was burned at the same time. Bale, as we have seen, was closely associated with Cromwell's reforms as part of his propaganda machine, and he had already been examined by Bishops Lee and Stokesley. He fled to the Low Countries upon Cromwell's fall, taking his family with him. In the *Catalogus* he speaks of the next years as the tyranny of the bishops, and the tenor of the prose works sustains this. There must be a possibility that the severity of Cromwell's fate and the threat to others left a mark upon Bale, making his subsequent robust and controversial writings more understandable.

He seems to have lived in Antwerp for about six years. It is not clear how he supported himself and his family, although it looks as though he lived in poverty.[18] He continued to try influencing religious affairs, mainly by producing prose works dealing with controversial topics. References to lost works attest this: *Apologia pro Barnes, Adversus Impostorem Standicium*, and *Pro Grayo contra Smithum* all concern particular people.[19] During that time many of his works appeared with false but unmistakably Protestant imprints: Geneva, Zurich, Basel, and Marburg (which had been used by Tyndale). Bale also used the pseudonyms "Henry Stalbridge" and "John Harrison." It is a paradox that he continued to support royal supremacy and to follow the Lutheran position that a truly Protestant monarch had absolute authority and should attract obedience. This loyalty is entwined with a thread of patriotism which runs through his work: he was always conscious of public affairs and sought to influence them. He had a sense of the special place of England in Christian history. He stuck to his Suffolk origins. While in exile he sometimes put Ipswich as the place of publication for his work: the *Summarium* appeared with two imprints, one labeled Wesel and the other Ipswich. Closely allied to his patriotism is his interest in history, especially the need to revise the chronicles—"I wolde wyshe some lerned Englyshe manne (as there are now most excellent fresh wyttes) to set forth the Englyshe chronycles in theyr ryght shape," (*Oldcastle*, fol. 5ᵛ).

However, the effect of this work was not approved by the English authorities, and his books were forbidden by royal proclamation in 1542.[20] From the king's point of view, Bale was going to do much worse after that date. In May 1546 the Privy Council ordered the Lord Mayor to investigate the importing of his work. By July it had become an offence to possess his books, and no printer was to print any book, ballad or play by him.[21] Shortly afterward, several titles were condemned, and it was proclaimed that they would be burned if discovered.[22]

Not much is known about the day-to-day events of Bale's life during this first exile, which lasted eight years, but he must have spent a great deal of time researching and writing. It is a period also of vigorous and active publication. What actually appeared may be divided into three categories: the literary history, the polemic and controversarial writings, and the dramatic works. But these cannot be strictly segregrated, and some works belong to more than one category.

Bale's work as a literary historian is probably his largest innovation during this time. Related to the patriotism mentioned above, it became a means of showing the many achievements of British writers. There is no doubt that Bale's Carmelite studies, as well as his labors with Leland, contributed to this work. A concern that the dissolution of the monasteries should not have the effect of destroying the accumulated libraries of the religious orders was something which he also shared with Leland, and which he now sought to help by the catalog of writers in the *Summarium* (1548). Much information about earlier English writers would now be lost if Bale had not set out to preserve it. He must have accumulated most of it during his travels. Moreover, he adapted and developed a method of presenting the biography of each author and a list of works in each case. This has preserved many titles and incipits of works now lost, and it was also set up in such a way that it could be added to as further details came to light. In the *Summarium* he actually asks readers to send him additional information.

Whatever Bale's ideological preoccupations, his attention to the accumulation of historical detail was exceptional. His work may not always be entirely reliable, but his working methods show a painstaking addition and modification of what he already knew. The *Summarium* is an enormous advance on the *Anglorum Heliades* in terms of scope and quantity. In the unpublished notebook, now known as the *Index Britanniae Scriptorum*, which dates from the years 1549 to 1557, he gave unique information about sources of data,[23] and in the *Catalogus* this process continued massively, providing evidence of a phenomenal energy on Bale's part.

It also seems likely that by the time of his first exile Bale had begun to collect books on his own account. Probably the monastic libraries were a significant source. It was during his search of the Carmelite library at Norwich in 1538 that he acquired the collection of documents about Wyclif known as the *Fasciculi Zizaniorum*.[24] He compiled an index to this collection, and in the same manuscript (Bodleian *MS e Musaeo 86*) he added the title *The Battayle of Johan Wycleffe* (*Bella Vuiclui*). In 1543, he also added a Latin translation of the *Examination of William Thorpe*.

In the biographies in the *Summarium*, Bale makes occasional comments about the nature and qualities of the works noted, but most of his observations reflect his polemical concerns. Alongside this, in other polemical writings, he made further use of what he had compiled about the history of the monastic orders. In particular he set out to expose and vilify the sexual mores of the monastic orders in *Votaries*. This depended upon a view of history in which, in broad outline, he presented the Church as having originally been pure but having become polluted as the papacy developed, particularly over the question of clerical celibacy. The essence of the contribution of Wyclif and the later Protestant reformers was that they were restoring to the true Church its original purity. Bale predicated this view of history upon the book of Revelation in his *Image*. The development of his own view of religious history was another highly significant process that was taking place at this time, and it was to have an influence upon a number of other writers.

Bale had already attacked and ridiculed the veneration of saints, identifying it particularly as an unscriptural practice. He seems to have decided, however, that if the Catholic saints were to be disregarded, the Protestant side would also need to create saints of its own. The essential difference was that any Christian who witnessed his faith could be seen as a saint. He set about illustrating this in his works on William Thorpe, John Oldcastle, and Anne Askew. The first two are part of his treatment of the older Wycliffite persecutions. The proceedings against Anne Askew have the urgency of contemporary outrage. Following her burning in 1546, Bale quickly produced two works: *The First Examination of Anne Askew* (1546) covered her interrogation in March 1545; and the *Latter Examination of Anne Askew* (1547) recounted her death. For these works he used her own testimony, which must have reached him through clandestine channels. He added a preface and a conclusion, as well as a running commentary. Stephen Gardiner, bishop of Winchester, was troubled to find at least four copies of the *First Anne Askew* in Winchester market in May 1547.[25]

Bale sustained and developed his polemical attacks in print in a number of differing ways during these years. He attacked the English bishops, especially Bonner and Gardiner in *A Man of Sin* (1543) and *The Epistle Exhortatory* (1544). *A Christian Exhortation unto Customable Swearers* (1543) was meant to discourage the taking of all kinds of oaths, especially those taken in youth which could not be sustained later. He celebrated Protestant qualities in his translation of *The True History of the Christian Departing of the Reverend Man D. Martin Luther* (1546) and in his editions of Princess Elizabeth's *Godly Meditation* (1548), extolling feminine virtues, and *A Treatise made by John Lambert* (1548; Lambert was burned in 1538).

He showed an interest in using poetry as a means of furthering polemical ideas in three works. *Rhithmi Vetustissimi* (1546) is an edition of a 200–year-old poem written by a Franciscan. An *Answer to a Papistical Exhortation* (1548) is written in verse attacking papistical ways. *A Mystery of Iniquity* (1545) publishes a poem by Ponce Pantolabus with a commentary by Bale exposing the folly of what is presented. This technique of commenting line by line on a text is used elsewhere, as in the scriptural commentary in *Image*. It seems that Bale's controversial work found a willing readership. Several of the works he wrote at this time were quickly reprinted.

His religious position involved an attack upon the devotion to the Virgin Mary, in sharp contrast to his own attitude when he was a Carmelite; he also wrote a vigorous denial of transubstantiation and of the sacrificial intent of the Mass. Like Luther, Bale stressed the faith of the individual Christian as against the false devotion of the priests who obscured the scripturally revealed Word of God by what he frequently referred to as "men's traditions."

It is difficult to tell how far Bale's interest in the drama developed during his period of exile. As in the case of his earlier journeys to France and the Netherlands, there is every possibility that he came into contact with a vigorous dramatic tradition. In the Low Countries this is the period of the *Rederijkersdrama*, especially the *Spelen van Sinne*, the allegorical plays of the Rhetoricians' Chambers which were performed at competitions in many towns and cities, and which have come down to modern times in very large numbers.[26] The performances were accessible to the public and took place in the open air, often at village fairs, or in cities like Antwerp, Ghent, and Bruges. It is unlikely that Bale missed these altogether, and it is possible to observe some similarities between his work and some features of the Dutch drama, a good deal of which was intensely Protestant in outlook and depended upon vigorous ridicule of human wickedness.

However, positive evidence that Bale took part in any performance eludes us. In the *Epistle Exhortatory* he complains that the authorities in England, presumably the bishops, were now persecuting players who were trying to persuade the people to worship God according to his holy laws, whereas formerly the players had not been accountable for any manner of blasphemy and impiety (fol. 18).

Bale must have spent time in preparing some of his plays for the press. In about 1546 he probably moved to Wesel in Germany, away from the risk of Catholic threat in the Netherlands. He made a contact with the Dutch Protestant printer, Dirk van der Straten, who now printed the *Three Laws* which had been listed in the *Anglorum Heliades* and must have been in existence before 1539. To these were added *John Baptist's Preaching* and *The Temptation of Our Lord*, printed as a consecutive and complementary pair, and *God's Promises*. All four plays appeared with a claim that they were compiled in 1538. Since we do not have copies which date earlier than 1547, it is not clear to what extent and when Bale carried out revisions. In the case of *Three Laws* some changes were certainly made after 1545. In the absence of any information about the publication of any other of his plays, we may suppose that Bale's intention in selecting these particular ones from his repertoire was to aim at a cyclic coherence, albeit a limited one, and also to pay attention to the life and ministry of Christ, especially in terms of Christ's role as a preacher. Apparently these plays had been written before Bale left England, and we should bear in mind that writing and performing plays may be a political act quite distinct from publishing them. Whatever the truth here, there is no doubt that the publication at a time when King Henry was nearing the end of his life must have had political implications for Bale. He may also have been looking now for patronage from England in the coming regime of King Edward, the new (Protestant) Josiah.

The list of plays in the *Summarium* indicates that Bale had also translated Thomas Kirchmayer's *Pammachius*. This play has some similarities to the eschatological themes of *Three Laws*, but direct influence is unlikely. As it happens, there was a performance of *Pammachius* at Christ's College, Cambridge, in 1545, to which Bishop Stephen Gardiner objected,[27] but there are no indications that Bale's translation was linked to this affair. The government's control over the performing of interludes in England had been much tightened during Bale's exile. There was legis-

lation in 1543 and 1544 by statute and proclamation forbidding interludes containing matter contrary to the teaching of the Church, and
confining even acceptable plays to the houses of noblemen. We may
understand "the teaching of the Church" to refer to doctrines of a more
traditional nature than those contained in Bale's plays.

Bishop

Bale may have waited a while before returning to England after
Edward's accession. Copies of the *Summarium* had contained an engrav-
ing which portrayed Bale presenting his book to the new king. We cannot be sure that this actually happened, but the picture is an indication
of Bale's expectations, especially as the picture had to be made for the
occasion. The political climate turned highly sympathetic to Protestantism with the ascendancy of Protector Somerset. Many of the restric-
tions on reading and performing were now removed.

However, it looks as though Bale's hopes of preferment were not ful-
filled for a while, perhaps because he had offended Principal Secretary of
State Sir William Paget over his vindication of Anne Askew. In personal
terms, however, Bale took an important step while living at Mountjoy
House, the home of the Countess of Richmond in Knightrider Street in
London.[28] There he met John Foxe, with whom he developed a working
relationship which was to last many years. Bale's influence is perceptible
in many respects in Foxe's *Acts and Monuments*—chiefly in that Bale's
sense of the martyrdom of English Protestants like Anne Askew was
shared by Foxe. Both men were essentially scholarly by temperament,
and both were interested in the accumulation of documentary evidence
to support their aims.

The *Summarium* had been intended to fill a gap in the history of
English writers, but now it became apparent that Leland would not be
able to complete the extensive work he had been preparing. While still
at Wesel, Bale had received copies of Leland's work and information
about his mental affliction. In 1549 he wrote an introduction, a conclusion, and a commentary on Leland's *New Year's Gift* (which had been presented to Henry VIII in 1546) and published it as *The Laborious Journey
and Search of John Leland for England's Antiquities*. His comments show
that he himself had been busily engaged in trying to record and recover
books, and he says that since his return form Germany he had visited
many libraries at Oxford, Cambridge, and London. He indicates that he
already has much to add to what was published in the *Summarium*. He

also visited booksellers at this time, perhaps a further indication that he was continuing to collect books on his own behalf.

Bale owed the first step in his next preferment to John Ponet, Bishop of Winchester. The Duke of Northumberland's seizure of power probably made this possible, as Bale acted as Ponet's chaplain for a time in 1551. He was given the rectorship of the parish of Bishopstoke, which lies on the Winchester side of Southampton. It appears that Bale resumed the writing of polemical pamphlets and the production of anti-Catholic drama. In 1552 he published *An Expostulation or Complaint against the Blasphemies of a Frantic Papist of Hampshire*. The work was dedicated to Northumberland, and in it Bale sought to expose the activities of an unregenerate papist priest who was continuing in his old ways. This theme became persistent in Bale's writings over the next few years. No doubt the change from one form of religion to another was neither simple nor consistent and there was, from Bale's point of view, much to complain about.[29]

In this work he is more specific about the drama, although the extent of his activities was not apparently as great as before the first exile. It appears that the same priest had reviled one of Bale's servants, who was learning a part in *Three Laws*, and this offender set about insulting Bale as well. The insult was for Bale a part of another theme which became important: that of the persecution of the righteous by the servants of Antichrist. We do not know whether the performance of *Three Laws* actually came to pass, or where Bale intended to have it performed, but the indication that Bale still retained the idea of using the stage for polemics is significant.

The next phase of Bale's life, his elevation to the bishopric of Ossory, is recounted in the *Vocation*, the largely autobiographical tract he wrote once he had made his escape from the dangerous situation in which he found himself—a situation which was no doubt partly of his own making. His account will be treated in more detail later, but here it is necessary to say that, although the *Vocation* contains much circumstantial detail which suggests that Bale was perhaps referring to a diary or to notes kept as events unfolded, the work is undoubtedly a deliberately managed version of events designed to vilify the Catholics and to underline his own sense that he was acting righteously. The fact that some of what happened to him could be made to appear as persecution supported his intention to show the hand of God in his deliverance. Hence he compares his journeys to those of St. Paul.

The narrative in the *Vocation* tells a well turned story. Bale heard that King Edward was coming to Southampton on a progress. On 15 August

1552, although Bale was sick, he set out from Bishopstoke on horseback to see Edward. Looking from a window, the king noticed Bale in the street. Being thus reminded that Bale was still alive (a comment perhaps meant as a protest at Bale's long wait for promotion), he commanded his officials to appoint Bale to the bishopric. It cannot have been as simple as this: no doubt the influence of Bale's friend John Philpot, a Protestant courtier later executed under Queen Mary, played a part in his preferment. Meticulously Bale gives a copy of the letter of appointment, which is signed by John Ponet (among others), the Bishop of Winchester who had already preferred him.

Bale claims to have put up token resistance on the grounds of ill health and old age, while really allowing it to appear that there was great determination in high places to send him to Ireland. No doubt the administration was keen to bring Ireland into the Protestant fold, and Bale's appointment was part of this policy. In December he left Bishopstoke with his books, and after a pause at Bristol he reached Waterford on 23 January 1553. He was immediately appalled by the papistical ways he found in Ireland. He indignantly introduces many anecdotes into the narrative, not forgetting to show how he righteously reacted to what he saw. He was consecrated in Dublin on 2 February 1553, according to the new Protestant rite upon which he insisted in spite of intense opposition. Two days later he became very ill and barely survived. His suspicion of poisoning was intensified by the death a few weeks later of the new Protestant Archbishop of Armagh, his friend Hugh Goodacre. In spite of his illness he preached the new religion during Lent in Kilkenny cathedral, and it is not surprising that he quickly encountered hostile responses. He expresses his horror in the *Vocation* about the respect shown to the illegitimate offspring of clerics, but he was unable to persuade any of his clergy to marry. He lets it appear that the local gentry were against him, including the influential Sellenger (St. Leger) family, and that they began a process designed to dispossess him of the house he lived in at Holmes Court.

Bale's narrative reaches a high point in the proclamation at Kilkenny of the "Lady Mary" as Queen of England, which he carefully dates as 20 August. For the occasion he refused to wear the cape and miter and to carry the crozier. Instead he carried the (New) Testament in his hand while his enemies, intent upon ritual, caused two priests to carry the miter and crozier before him. After his sermon Bale made use of his plays once again, perhaps as a response to what he called the pageants of the Catholic ritual. The young men performed his *God's Promises*, with music, in the morning, and *John Baptist's Preaching* and the *Temptation of Our Lord* in the afternoon.

Bale's narrative of these and the following events is punctuated by apparently verbatim details of what he said to his enemies, as well as what he said in his sermons to reprove their beliefs and their behavior. Not much of what he said is notable for its tact, and it is not surprising that the reactions against him intensified as the intention to restore traditional doctrine and practices developed under Queen Mary. After the murder of five of his servants who were mowing on a holy day, 8 September 1553, and various other threats to his safety, Bale and his wife fled from their residence at Holmes Court, first to Kilkenny and thence to Dublin. He left behind his books, which amounted, he claimed later, to two cartloads.

Bale intended to make his escape to Scotland, but in the following sequence of events, closely narrated in the *Vocation*, he seems to have been prone to accident. Boarding one boat, he was seized by the Flemish captain of another, abetted by a pilot called Walter; Bale identifies him as a "Pylate." Deprived of his goods and money, Bale was virtually a prisoner during a complicated voyage which took him first to St. Ives in Cornwall, after gales had blown the ship back to Waterford.

In Cornwall Bale was allowed ashore and found time to be scandalized by the papistical ways of the inhabitants. He managed to escape a charge of heresy at the local court but had to pursue the captain in a boat provided by "another Judas," as the former tried to leave him behind, having taken possession of all Bale's valuables. The captain went privateering unsuccessfully on his own account with Bale still on board. Next Bale was taken to Dover, where another attempt was made to give him up to the authorities for profit. Bale managed to talk himself out of this threat by offering money to be paid by friends in the Low Countries as a ransom. Perhaps collecting such a ransom is what the captain had intended in any case. Once this new bargain was struck, the ship set sail for the Netherlands. Bale was duly released, after three weeks in confinement awaiting the raising of the ransom. During this time there was a possibility that he might be sent back to the Marian authorities in London. Bale saw it as providential that the local inquisitor of heretics, "a cruel monk" from Louvain, was ill during the whole time of his imprisonment.

This account is given in great detail, apparently reflecting the actuality of events. Throughout, it reads like a piece of fiction, and this impression is intensified because Bale manages events to show the righteousness of his conduct, the persecution he suffered, and the divine concern for his well-being. Bale immediately set about publishing his account of these events in order to make polemical gain. The central message was that Protestant England, now experiencing persecution under the yoke of Queen Mary, should not despair. The colophon impertinently claims that the book was "Imprinted in Rome / before the castell of S. Angell / at the signe of S. Peter in Decembre / Anno D. 1553." In fact, the printer's mark is that of Hugh Singleton, who probably printed the book at Wesel in the following year.

Second Exile

Although the *Vocation* contains much detailed factual information about what happened to Bale, its chief purpose is to demonstrate the risk of persecution and martyrdom which Bale felt now threatened Protestants. In this objective he draws near to the work of John Foxe. During Bale's second exile, Bale and Foxe worked closely together, probably collaborating in some way over Foxe's preparation of *Commentarii Rerum in Ecclesia Gestarum* which appeared at Strasbourg in 1554. This work also turns toward the subject of martyrdom and the deeds of earlier Christians like Wyclif, who might be held to have anticipated Protestantism.[30]

There was some reaction against the *Vocation* in Marian England, not least because of Bale's analogy between his journeys and St. Paul's.[31] Bale attacked the Catholic administration once more by publishing a translation of Stephen Gardiner's *De Vera Obedientia*. This work had first appeared in 1535 during Cromwell's ascendancy, designed by its author to support King Henry's authority against the pope. By publishing a translation Bale sought to embarrass Gardiner, who was now influentially situated as Mary's Lord Chancellor. The place of publication was allegedly "Roane" (for Rouen or Rome), and the translator was Michael Wood. However, Hugh Singleton's printer's mark appears in the book, and it is thus a companion to the *Vocation*.[32] Perhaps as a result of this venture, there was a royal proclamation in June 1555 banning Bale's books once more. According to Foxe, William Tyms, one of six martyred at Smithfield on 24 April 1556, confessed to agreeing with *De Vera Obedientia*, and with *Image*.[33]

It seems that Bale went to Strasbourg for a while after escaping from Ireland. From there was published in 1554 (also bearing Hugh Singleton's mark) a work which has been attributed to him: *The Resurrection of the Masse*, allegedly by Hugh Hilarie. Written in quatrains, this has the Masse as its principal speaker, and it proceeds ironically to praise many doctrines which Bale had elsewhere condemned, such as auricular confession and prayers for souls in purgatory. Eventually Masse is denounced by a simple maid called Communion.

Bale's second exile took place in rather different circumstances from the first. In 1540 the number of exiles had been much smaller. Now the severity of the Marian regime meant that exiles with a much wider spectrum of views were finding places of refuge in Continental towns and cities. Foxe estimates the total at about 800. One of these communities was at Frankfurt-on-Main, where in June 1554 the concentration of distinguished English exiles was so great that the authorities, encouraged by Philip Melanchthon, allowed them to form their own congregation. Bale, still probably at Strasbourg, was one of four candidates proposed by the community there as minister for Frankfurt. He apparently then moved to Frankfurt, but shortly afterwards he signed a letter, along with others, asking John Knox to take up the position.

The result was a deep division in the congregation at Frankfurt. Knox, once he arrived, found support for a further reform of Cranmer's 1552 *Prayer Book*. Bale and others, including Richard Cox, one of the commissioners who had set up the *Prayer Book* originally, wanted to use it unchanged. Bale's support for this is in line with his insistence upon the Protestant rite at his consecration in Kilkenny Cathedral. His position in terms of the spectrum had always had certain conservative elements, as his condemnation of the Anabaptists in the 1530s had revealed. Now, in the face of a more radical approach he sided with the moderates. In March 1555 an appeal was made to Calvin, and Knox eventually withdrew, leaving the conservative group with the upper hand. But Bale also left for Basel, probably in November, following Foxe, who had deprecated the dispute and tried to sustain a neutral stance. The troubles at Frankfurt continued for some time after Bale left. Indeed, he felt them deeply and claimed that they followed him to Basel.[34] He admired instead the comparative peace at Geneva. He matriculated at the University of Basel for the year 1555–56. He also resumed contact with Conrad Gesner, the bibliographer to whom he subsequently dedicated part of the *Catalogus*. Meanwhile in England Bale's books were again condemned to the flames.[35]

Bale and Foxe probably took up residence in the Clarakloster, a former convent where a number of English exiles lived, and made contact with John Oporinus, the Protestant publisher. Foxe worked for him as a reader, and possibly Bale did the same. Both were now deeply engaged in writing: Foxe worked on the *Acts and Monuments*, and Bale on the *Catalogus*. It seems likely that each influenced the other. There are certainly places, like the treatment of Anne Askew, where the two seem to have used the same documents. Both works show enormous authorial energy and a disposition to see divine influence in human affairs, especially in a Protestant direction. Though differences are discernible, the two authors share a concern to read and construct history according to Protestant ideology.

In Bale's case the accumulation of information over many years now reached fruition with a vast expansion of the work in the *Summarium*. It is a remarkable achievement that, in spite of all the vicissitudes, he maintained a continuous application to this project. Somehow he managed to retain his notebooks and to expand them enormously. He extended his study to cover Ireland, Scotland, and the Hebrides. The *Catalogus* finally comprised 14 centuries (the authors were grouped in hundreds, as in the *Summarium*). The book went to press in its first state in 1557, before the death of Mary, and some copies were issued. However, Mary's death and the accession of Elizabeth in 1558 led to further authorial intervention. Bale inserted into some copies on 4 March 1559 a dedication to Elizabeth in which among other things he returns to an old motif found in the *Godly Meditation* and *Anne Askew*: the praise of good and holy women. One of the expansions in the *Catalogus* was the insertion, in some breaks between individual biographies, of a continuous but anecdotal history of the papacy and its offences. This largely embodied the historical structure developed in *Image*. The items in this sequence were extracted and collected as *Acta Romanorum Pontificum* and published by Oporinus in 1558. This work may have been a kind of homage to Bale's long-dead colleague, Robert Barnes, who had published *Vitae Pontificum Romanorum*, a work with somewhat similar objectives, at Wittenberg in 1535.[36] In his preliminaries Bale thanks Calvin and Melanchthon for their hospitality during his exile. Like the *Summarium*, the *Catalogus* and the *Acta* were written in Latin, a decision which suggests a desire on Bale's part to reach an international audience.

Retirement

Bale returned to England in the summer of 1559, having seen the *Catalogus* through the press. At the age of sixty-three, after many years of struggle and some poverty, he was now in ill health. He was probably not willing to resume his exacting duties in Ossory, although for a while he still had the title of bishop. He was admitted to a canonry at Canterbury Cathedral on 10 February 1560, receiving a stipend of about £40 a year. This was patronage of a kind, but in subsequent correspondence his continuing plea of poverty suggests that he felt himself insufficiently recognized.

He tried to resume his studies and, to an extent, his dramatic work. As on previous occasions, he seems to have been eminent enough to attract some royal attention. Queen Elizabeth wrote to the Sellenger family in Ireland requesting the return of his lost collection of books. It appears that she expected he would resume his attempt to write the history of England. But there was no satisfactory response about the books and manuscripts Bale had accumulated. Bale wrote, again unavailingly, to Matthew Parker, now archbishop of Canterbury, on 30 July 1560, making it clear that of the "two great wayne loades"—he lists more than 350 manuscript titles, let alone incunabula—the Sellenger family had kept the most part, some in Ireland and some in Kent. Bale sent Parker a few small manuscripts with this letter in which he himself raised the question of the "perfourmance of an Englysh chronycle which I have begonne and not fynyshed." The collection has never been fully traced, although some of the books have turned up. Bale himself recovered a few in Kent. Parker acquired some of them on Bale's death, and they are to be found in the library he donated to Corpus Christi College in Cambridge.[37]

Bale's international reputation was high. Matthias Flacius Illyricus in his *Historia Ecclesiastica* (Magdeburg, 1560–74) shows the influence of Bale's *Image*. After Bale's death, Parker loaned Flacius some of his manuscripts. It has been suggested that Bale's letter to Parker, mentioned above, was a response from an inquiry by Flacius which had reached Parker from the queen's secretary.[38] Flacius offered to arrange the publication of Bale's work at Wittenburg or Leipzig. During the second exile Bale claimed to have worked with Flacius on the production of two works, although the extent of his contribution was not great. Probably Bale's work was most useful because of the amount of information it contained. The significance of his ideological influence will be considered later in this book.

There is little sign of the continuation of Bale's polemical work after his return to England. Perhaps, with the Elizabethan settlement of the religious controversy, the battle was now over—at least for a time. However, in 1561 Bale did bring out his *Declaration of Bonner's Articles*, a work he had written during the exile in Basel. His hostility to the Catholic bishops had not diminished. In similar vein he objected in 1560

to the hanging of the arms and cardinal's hat of Reginald Pole, Mary's
archbishop of Canterbury, in the cathedral at Canterbury. He also wrote
an unpublished reply to criticism of the *Vocation*.[39]

Image and *Votaries* were reprinted in 1560. The latter was also pub-
lished in a French edition at Geneva in 1561 and at Lyon in 1563. After
Bale's death John Studley translated the *Acta Romanorum Pontificum* as
The Pageant of Popes in 1574.

With regard to drama, Bale revised the text of *King Johan*. It has been
assumed that this was for a performance at Ipswich, which the Queen
visited in 1561. The manuscript is said to have emerged from there in
the nineteenth century, but other local evidence from Suffolk is lacking.
Although a performance may never have taken place, the manuscript
itself has been substantially altered and added to by Bale in his own
hand. As we shall see in more detail later, it is clear that the long passage
for the ending, which he transcribed in revision on smaller paper than
the original version dating from the 1530s, is continuous in regard to
both handwriting and paper. Because it contains a reference to
Elizabeth, the section containing this adjustment must have been made
after 1558. However, the autograph corrections to the earlier part of the
manuscript are often matters of spelling and punctuation, and it is likely
that these were done with printing rather than performance in mind.
Attention to the mechanics of productions in the stage directions is perfunctory in these late additions, whereas the earlier text had shown close
attention to some aspects of production. There is supporting evidence for
this view of Bale's intentions, inasmuch as his *Three Laws* was reprinted
in London in 1562.

On the other hand, an incident which has recently come to light sug-
gests that Bale may have been contemplating dramatic activity in
Canterbury. One Hugh Pilkington stated in a dispute which arose in
Canterbury on 24 May 1560 that a friar's garment was being made by
Hugh Johns because "Mr. Bale setteth forth a play wherein there's a
priest."[40] Such a garment would have suited an evil character such as
Dissimulation or Sedition in *King Johan*, Hypocrisy in *Three Laws*, or
Satan in *Temptation*. The revisions to *King Johan* included many careful
emendations to the prosody—which may point to performance, to pub-
lication, or to both.

Another incident, without significance for the drama, occurred in
October 1560, when John Okeden accused Bale of being an Anabaptist
and a heretic, in a row with Bale's son John. The subsequent lawsuit vindicated Bale on 17 June 1561.

These events give glimpses of Bale and his reputation in his last years at Canterbury. He died on 15 November 1563 and was buried in the nave of the cathedral. Dorothy was to receive an annuity from the cathedral funds, by royal command, for at least another six years. In the year of Bale's death, John Foxe published his *Acts and Monuments*, a work which embodies the results of many of Bale's labors. The book's subsequent popularity in Protestant England indicates that Bale had been close to the fundamental origins of the Reformation in England—indeed that he was one of its creators, certainly in a purely physical sense, but more significantly in the ideas he developed and propagated.

Chapter Two

Polemical Writings: Prose—and Some Verse

An Outline of Bale's Theology

The main purpose of this chapter is to outline John Bale's views as they appeared in the prose works. His views may then be used in commenting on his works of literary history and bibliography, as well as in shedding light on the plays. In the process it should be possible to discuss the nature and purpose of his nondramatic writings, which are primarily involved in religious controversy. Finally, his verse must also be considered.

It will be clear from chapter 1 that the chronology of the plays is not easy to determine. Of those that survive, *Three Laws* is possibly the earliest, followed by parts of the manuscript of *King Johan*; these were apparently in existence by the middle of 1538, and almost certainly they originated some years before. The three surviving biblical plays were probably written after the other two, in spite of the claim on the title pages that they were compiled in 1538: they may not, however, be very much later. These, as well as *Three Laws*, were printed at Wesel in 1547 or 1548, leaving up to 10 years for modifications to be made before they were established in the form we now have them. Some of the alterations to the *King Johan* manuscript were certainly made after 1558. Thus it is possible that the plays may give us an insight into Bale's position in the 1530s, before the polemical prose and verse were written, but caution is necessary: the extent to which they were modified later by the views and attitudes expressed in his prose works of the 1540s is problematic.

As to the prose, with the exception of the manuscript *Answer to Certain Articles*, which can be dated 1537, all the rest are apparently later in origin than the plays, and most were written in the 1540s during the first exile. When this exile began, Bale was 45 years old. The next few years were prolific. Although he had not apparently been in a powerful political position at home, he had certainly been aware of public and doctrinal issues. Henry VIII's stance at this time turned on the Six

Articles of June 1539. These had been constructed in response to a need to reduce pressure against Protestantism from the Continental powers, which became particularly menacing after the concord between Francis I of France and Emperor Charles V at Aigues-Mortes in France. Apart from this, Henry had always retained a pro-Catholic tendency.[1] Perhaps the most significant items in the Six Articles were the reaffirmations of transubstantiation and auricular confession. It seems likely that after the fall of Thomas Cromwell it became essential to Bale, who was living in exile for fear of persecution from the conforming or tradition-minded bishops, to continue to sustain opposition against such items as these.

The Reformation in Bale's terms was incomplete, and indeed it is clear that the acceptance of a change in doctrine was by no means universal, nor indeed was it complete in many individuals who apparently conformed to the new doctrines. There was still a considerable propaganda battle to be fought: the targets were those in power, especially the King and his bishops, but also a wider readership of ordinary people. The preaching role, essential as a means of communication to the new Protestant ministry, could now be supplemented by a print culture derived from and related to the earnest study of the Bible. Many might now respond more and more to a printed output in compendious forms. Cromwell, partly at his own expense, had striven to make the vernacular Bible accessible from 1538.[2] Bishop Stephen Gardiner expressed his indignation that copies of *The First Examination of Anne Askew* turned up in the Winchester market, presumably in the shadow of his own cathedral. These factors perhaps help to account for the vigor of Bale's subsequent output: his surviving works include 10 books printed at Antwerp between 1543 and 1548, and five, plus four plays, at Wesel by Dirk van der Straten. During this period, however, Bale retained an allegiance to King Henry, whom he presents as a godly and heroic monarch. Yet it is clear that Bale's works were read by people in power, especially Bishop Bonner who ensured that some were burned in public in 1546.

There is extensive exposition of Bale's views in these works, and we can say that in comparison with the plays, there is some development and variety. Fundamentally, however, his views were similar throughout these works, and many themes are expressed in both prose and plays. There is, in fact, a kind of circularity here because Bale tended deliberately to reiterate or restate his views.

While it will be necessary to say something about his developing theological position, it should be noted that a good deal of his polemical prose, and some of his verse, is directed toward specific situations, whether national or personal, and that it is somewhat artificial to draw a line between theology and politics at this point in English history. Most of Bale's publications have a specific political context which we are sometimes in a position to discern; and this is true of the plays, even of the putative multiple creation of *King Johan*.

Before considering the nature of the individual works of controversy, it may be helpful to give a general view of Bale's theological position. Almost all the aspects to be mentioned may be found in the teaching of Wyclif and his followers who undoubtedly became a major influence upon Bale, and one to whom Bale himself accorded the highest status, even though, to begin with, he may have turned more directly to, and been more influenced by, his contemporaries Tyndale and Barnes.[3] It is somewhat difficult to ascertain whether he used Luther's work directly. He was obviously very competent in Latin, but the quality of his German remains unclear even though he lived in German-speaking communities from time to time. The principal exception to the many topics in the Wycliffite precedents is the doctrine of justification by faith (*sola fides*) which was propounded by Luther in *The Freedom of a Christian* (1520) and elsewhere; it is a doctrine which is linked by him closely to the rejection of the dependence upon good works:

> For the person is justified and saved, not by works or laws, but by the Word of God, that is, by the promise of his grace, and by faith, that the glory may remain God's, who saved us not by works of righteousness that we have done, but by virtue of his mercy by the word of his grace when we believed.[4]

In line with Wycliffite teaching, Luther also held that the faith of a Christian was to be directed solely to Christ and not to the Virgin or to saints in general (*solus Christus*). A third principle, also found in Wyclif and Luther, but widely disseminated, was that the Word of God was of primary significance (*sola scriptura*). This led to the important question of the vernacular Bible, and also to worship in the vernacular. Many of these points were emphasized by Tyndale.

Luther scrutinized the role of the papacy. Although he claimed in the dedication of *The Freedom of a Christian* to Leo X that there was nothing personal in his attacks, his criticism of the avarice of the papacy is a dominating theme, and one which Bale followed. But Bale put the emphasis more upon the papal encouragement of sexual failings of the clergy, which he portrayed vehemently and sensationally in the *Acts of*

English Votaries and in the *Acta Romanorum Pontificum*. For the latter Barnes's *Vitae Romanorum Pontificum* (1535) was undoubtedly influential: there are places where Bale seems to be relying upon Barnes verbatim, though this is not to say that Bale did not add a great deal of his own material. This attack was also directed against the monastic vows of celibacy and against the prohibition of clerical marriage. Here Bale was inclined to take an historical view which emphasized that these things were not scriptural. In *Image* and *Votaries* he traced the stages by which he thought the papacy tightened the rules in this respect. His view of marriage was that God blessed it in the Garden of Eden. The changes were brought about, in his view, by the avarice of the papacy, as noted by Luther, who claimed that everything, even heaven, was up for sale.

The alleged profligacy of the papacy was not, however, its chief fault for Bale, but an index of the unremitting and unquenchable evil within. Like Wyclif he characterized the pope as Antichrist, deriving this concept ultimately from the book of Revelation, although there were medieval and contemporary influences. The historical failure of the papacy in its introduction of celibacy was compounded by Sylvester II's summoning of Satan by means of necromancy whereby he was released from Hell in the year 1000. This led to an elaboration of ceremony and ritual which was a frequent object of Bale's ridicule. The particular objects of attack were Church music, formulaic language, and the elaborate vestments. These he characterized with various metaphors suggesting falseness, juggling, and playing a part in a play. The worship of the saints would damage the value of Christ's promise by obscuring its sufficiency. Thus came the ridicule of individual saints, especially St. Thomas à Becket. Becket was proclaimed a traitor in 1538, his reputation having been attacked by Tyndale and Cromwell. Similarly, though repentance was important, there was little value in the confessional. Bale made this out to be a threat to national security, being a means of propagating sedition under the secrecy required in auricular confession. With Luther, Bale saw everyman as his own priest as far as spiritual matters were concerned. The function of the ministry was to follow the example of Christ in preaching the Word, even though this brought the risk of persecution and death, following again the example of the Saviour.

Although Bale's surviving early work shows little interest in discussing the patristic writings, he obviously knew and collected them extensively, as his list of lost books indicates. In the prose works he reveals some thoughts about which of them supported the true Church and which perverted it. Indeed the perverters of God's word became a

major preoccupation for him.[5] The practices which he saw as evil were
connected with this evaluation of the traditional authorities. He questioned, therefore, the nature of the Mass, doubting its significance as a
recurring sacrifice, and rejecting the belief in transubstantiation. Like
Tyndale he accepted the idea of Christ's Last Supper because it was scriptural, but the Mass was not.[6] The criticism of pardoners and of the indul-
gences which they brought, along with the worship of relics, went back
beyond Chaucer. It was taken up by Wyclif, and, indeed, it became one
of the identifying marks of proto-Protestantism for the fifteenth and sixteenth centuries, even though Erasmus and Sir Thomas More, bringing
in an infusion of humanism which may also have influenced Luther, had
both doubted the value of these practices. Alongside this went the condemnation of pilgrimages, also questioned but not rejected by Erasmus
in the *Colloquies*.[7]

But these outward practices, though they attracted his scorn, seem to
have been less troubling to Bale than the doctrine of Purgatory, which
exercised many of his contemporaries. Bale had to reject this because,
once again, it implied the insufficiency of Christ's promise of salvation
for those with faith. Nor did he accept that it was possible to better the
state of the dead by intercession, or by the accumulation of good works
with this in mind. Luther had made it clear that good works like fasting
need not be condemned in themselves, but only if they were pursued as
a kind of spiritual barter, instead of being the outward sign of inner
goodness: Bale followed this doctrine closely.

Patriotism is very much part of Bale's religious stance. As we shall see
in his historical works, he had a strong sense of the continuity of
Christianity in the British Isles from its purest origins in apostolic times,
to the extent that he regarded these islands as uniquely preserving the
truth which other nations had lost. In the 1530s the question of royal
supremacy emerged as an important part of the Protestant outlook.
There is no doubt that Luther had contributed to this, especially in his
Address to the Christian Nobility where he enjoined upon the German
rulers and princes the need to resist the papacy. This view is extended by
Bale to a distinctly hierarchical attitude to the ranks of society.[8] Bale's
historical view shows his belief that the papacy had continued to seek to
undermine English kings, notably King John and Richard II. This patriotic viewpoint of course underpins his hostility to auricular confession
and to interference, as he saw it, by the papacy in English or British
affairs. One thing to bear in mind is that, in the exigencies of political
maneuvering, issues such as this could be seen as very urgent, and this is

particularly so in the period before the fall of Cromwell when there was much to play for in gaining influence over Henry.

Even though Henry VIII's traditional policies after the fall of Cromwell were very much against many of the ideas discussed here, Bale sustained his loyalty to the monarchy and refrained from making invidious comparisons when the more congenially Protestant regime of Edward, who was presented as a new Josiah, would take over, a time much anticipated by Bale during his first exile. There emerges in his work a sense of the heroism of those resisting the papacy, and Bale turned this in some cases into a martyrdom, even though his attitude toward martyrdom was specifically designed to avoid a worship of the miraculous. This is embodied in his strong sense that what believers actually said in response to adversity, whether verbal examination or torment, was of great value and needed to be preserved.

A great deal of Bale's writing was concerned with the reinterpretation of history. In the political stress of the 1530s it had become necessary to provide some precedent for the King's actions and also for the developing momentum of Protestant belief. It may also have been a priority to create historical justification for current beliefs and practices. In the *Three Laws*, which may be Bale's earliest extant play, Bale had taken over a tripartite view of history which divided it into three periods: the Law of Nature, the Law of Moses, and the Law of Christ. This structure can be found in St. Paul and St. Augustine; it became a part of medieval thinking, as can be seen in the *Speculum Sacerdotale*.[9] It had the strong advantage for the Protestants that it could be derived from the Bible. Tyndale, who was probably influential on Bale's thinking at the time of the conception of *Three Laws*, divided the Bible into the Law and the Gospel.[10] The Gospel embodied Christ's promise of salvation which would respond to the faith of the individual Christian. The quotation above, from Luther's *Freedom of a Christian*, makes clear the link between this view and justification by faith alone.

This pattern of thinking underpinned the promise made for the Christian at baptism, and it was part of the covenant made by Christ with his people. It showed itself also in the view that these vows were made once and for all and did not need repeating or indeed echoing in the superfluous vows made by men and women entering religious orders. It also related to the doctrine of the Elect, which appears somewhat rarely in Bale's writings.[11] The importance of this doctrine to Protestants was that it countered the idea of free will, which in its turn left open the Roman sense of the efficacy of intercession for the departed.

As we have noted, *Three Laws* may have been revised after 1545, before it was printed. It was at this period that a significant development took place in Bale's view of history. The new view was still meant to serve the same ends, but it offered a response to the changing circumstances of Henry VIII's later years. Possibly the lead came from Luther who read the book of Revelation as a prophecy of the Reformation. I shall leave a detailed discussion of Bale's newer thinking to the point below where the *Image of Both Churches* is considered. Here it is perhaps sufficient to say that he embodied his tripartite view into one containing seven ages deriving the outline from the opening of the seven seals in Revelation. This scheme placed contemporary events in a biblical framework and perhaps brought comfort in the difficult time of the first exile when many hopes were at risk. In this respect the Bible was seen as something to be decoded. To further the decoding, Bale elaborated the notion of the two churches: one enlightened by the Gospel and the other contaminated by what he usually referred to as "men's traditions," signifying for him the prolonged historical distortion of the truth by the papacy. This view of history did indeed lead to further vilification of the papacy. To intensify this, Bale elaborated and reiterated the idea that Satan was imprisoned at the Resurrection for a thousand years, and that it was only the evil, and the necromancy, of the popes which allowed Satan to be loosed once more upon the world. This brought in the worst period of the Church's history, from Bale's point of view, that of papal domination in what we now call the late Middle Ages—for him the age of locusts. The importance placed upon the Word made the question of blasphemy an urgent one, and it accounts for the attacks he made on what he considered to be false sects and perverters of the Word.

As it happens there are passages in *Three Laws* which suggest Bale was moving toward this apocalyptic view of history:

> The apostle Johan in the Apocalyps doth saye
> He sawe a newe heaven and a newe earth aperynge,
> The olde earth and sea were taken cleane awaye:
> That heaven in mannys fayth, that earth hys understandynge.[12]

It is possible, of course, that such passages may have been added in revision to take account of these new preoccupations.

One historical theme which Bale did elaborate in the 1540s was his concern for martyrdom. We have seen that he accepted the Protestant criticism of the intercession of the saints. This led to a denial of the value of many saints; only a few, such as the apostles or those reflecting the qualities of the original and pure Church, were now admitted. In their place, however, it became necessary to create and celebrate Protestant worthies who were able to reveal the Word in their lives, and who were able to proceed without the superstitious foregrounding of miracles which was anathema to Bale. This was achieved by reviving some of the key figures of Wycliffite history, especially John Oldcastle and William Thorpe, and by identifying a new contemporary martyr in Anne Askew, who was the victim not so much of the king as of the tyrannous bishops in England. In this activity Bale may have taken a lead from William Tyndale's *Testament of William Tracie*, published at Antwerp in 1535. Bale's historical work became an important and fruitful part of Protestant history and led in time to Bale's having some influence on John Foxe's *Acts and Monuments*.

Individual Works: Prose and Verse

Within the outline we have just sketched above, it is possible to consider Bale's handling of broad principles in particular works. It will be evident that Bale uses a number of specific literary devices and rhetorical methods, and also has an ability to exploit the strategies of publication in order to extend the influence and effectiveness of his works. Some of these would be regarded as traditional literary devices, such as alliteration, amplification, and repetition; others we can now perceive from a more modern conception of book production as part of ideological methodology.

While it is not desirable to schematize Bale's polemical works too strictly, it is convenient to deal with them in terms of three broad objectives. One is his perception of holy people whose work and lives he approved. This preoccupation was no doubt a response to the traditional worship of the saints which he came to dislike intensely after his conversion. A second group is centered on particular attacks on individual circumstances or characters. Sometimes these may be a response to particular political needs, for Bale was aware of the threats posed by public or royal policies, whether ostensibly sympathetic to Protestant aims or directly opposed to them. A third group embodies central doctrinal concerns and seeks to elaborate them. Works in the other two categories naturally share these doctrines, but as well as being concerned with particular circumstances, Bale was also interested in constructing a body of doctrine which was based upon the gathering and presentation of historical or anecdotal evi-

dence. The central works here are *Image* and *Votaries* which are the fruits
of extensive research, some of it carried out before the conversion and
now made to play a new role. It appears, to judge from the number of
reprints, that these two works were among his most popular. In addition, the perception of abuses leads Bale to hammer insistently against
the taking of vows in *Customable Swearers* and in his *Apology*, and against
the Mass in *Resurrection* and elsewhere.[13]

These categories suggest that Bale had a number of different authorial
intentions. With very few exceptions, however, we find many of the doctrinal elements, not to mention the anecdotes, reappearing in different
contexts. Much of the material also appears in the plays and in the bibliographical works to be considered in chapter three. The research for these
works no doubt continued at the same time as the polemical writing.

Although Bale had a particular animus against the worship of saints,
largely because he scorned miracles as a means of generating faith, it was
necessary to evolve respect and admiration for the people who sustained
the Protestant cause, not least because they could be seen as carrying out
the will of God, and also because they were considered to be examples of
God's elect. Bale found many minor and apparently orthodox figures to
whom he could extend his approval—"Yet denye I it not but some godly
men were amonge them in those dayes"—and he goes on to mention
Bede and Alcuin among others. John Wyclif he hailed as the morning
star of the Reformation, but apart from substantial items in the
Summarium and the *Catalogus*, Bale did not write a work devoted to him.
His account of King Johan was partly oriented toward showing him as a
saintly king, and indeed one who was martyred in God's service. In the
Epistle Exhortatory (1544) he gives a list of more than 20 honest martyrs,
some famous like Tyndale and Barnes, but many obscure (xiii[r-v]).

In the prose works the most extensive treatment was afforded to Sir
John Oldcastle, the fifteenth-century Lollard (also known as Lord
Cobham), and to Anne Askew, whose conviction for heresy and death at
the stake in 1546 made her a contemporary heroine and martyr. It is
notable in both instances that Bale makes a point of using primary documents relating to the proceedings against both victims. This reflects the
importance he attached to the witnessing of events he considered to be
of divine importance; it also shows one of his commonest stances as an
author, that of a compiler, or perhaps in modern terminology, editor: one
who collects, arranges, and comments upon material derived from the
work of others. He makes a point of telling readers that he has translated the documents from "barbarous Latin."[14]

There was some difficulty in adopting the rather dubious activities of Oldcastle as a hero, since he was rebel and became involved in a number of shady actions. However, Bale was impressed partly because Oldcastle had caused some of Wyclif's works to be copied (*Laborious Journey*, sig. A7ᵛ). He also happened to have some very usable documentation at hand, which could be made to vilify the interrogators. Some of it is known to us in the *Fasciculi Zizaniorum*, a Carmelite collection in manuscript which Bale probably acquired in 1538 when he was working for Leland, before his exile. It contained the account of the trial by Thomas Walden, the Carmelite confessor of King Henry IV. He may also have used an account by Tyndale.

Much of the text of *John Oldcastle* is in direct speech, with added commentary by Bale, and it appears that Bale was using the record of the trial verbatim. Since the trial had occurred in 1417, there was ample scope for Bale to change things to suit himself, and we cannot be sure that he has not in fact done so. However, the apparent directness of the language suits Bale's purpose very well. Its dramatic nature is enhanced by the references to laughter and anger that accompany some of the speeches. The account is subdivided into separated documents, and given subheadings such as "The Christian Belief of the Lord Cobham," "The Determination [i.e., Judgment] of the Archbishop and Clergy," and, most telling, "An [not "The"] Abjuration Counterfeited of [i.e., by] the Bishops" (46). His commentary includes a summary of narrative details, as well as doctrinal comments, such as a parallel between the death of Oldcastle and the crucifixion, and a contrast between the virtue of Oldcastle at his execution and the viciousness, according to Bale, of Thomas à Becket at his murder (55–56).[15] Bale's commentary also seeks to discredit the contemporary accounts of the trial by showing up inconsistencies. The marginal notes, which are presumably his rather than the printer's and are always an important feature of Bale's prose works, sustain the hostility of the commentator:

> Ye lie, ye knaves, ye lie . . .
> How prove ye that by scripture? (47)
> Never came this abjuration to the hands of the Lord Cobham. (48)

However, some of Bale's marginal notes are more objective references to the authorities he is using.

The two works relating to Anne Askew had the special feature of seeming more immediate, and indeed more sensational, by virtue of their

very contemporaneity. She came from the Lincolnshire gentry—"a gentyl
woman very yonge, dayntye and tender" (*First Anne Askew*, sig. v)—and
in 1545 she was questioned about her views on the sacrament by Bonner,
the Bishop of London, and a target dear to Bale. Probably she produced a
statement on this occasion which was acceptable to the authorities and
led to her release, but in the following year she was again questioned; as
she proved obdurate, she was tried and condemned. More sensationally,
because it was suspected that she might have had connections among
Protestant ladies at court, gathered around Queen Catherine Parr, she
was tortured on the rack personally by the Lord Chancellor—to no
avail—before being burned on 16 July 1546. It looks as though it was
her death which stimulated Bale to action, for he produced *The First
Examination of Anne Askew* in November of that year, and this was followed by *The Latter Examination of Anne Askew* in January of 1547. Both
of these works were printed by Dirk van der Straten in Wesel. In both
volumes Bale again makes the claim that he is working from original documents, in this case apparently written by Anne herself:

> Two examynacyons . . . whom she sent abroade by her owne hande
> wrytyng.

and:

> whose lattre handelynge here foloweth in course, lyke as I receyved it in
> coppye by serten duche merchauntes commynge from thens whych had
> bene at their burnynge, and beholden the tyrannouse vyolence there
> shewed. First out of the preson she wrote unto a secrete frynde of hers
> after thys maner folowynge.[16]

The bulk of the text is again arranged in distinct documents, such as
"The summe of the condemnacyon of me Anne Askew at Yeldehawle"
(sig. D8); "My lettre sent to the lord Chauncellour" (sig. E3ᵛ); "The
effect of my examynacyon and handelynge sens my departure from
Newgate" (sig. E6); "The confessyon of her faythe whych Anne afterwards made in Newgate afore she suffered" (sig. G6). The change of pronoun in the last, however, suggests that Bale's editing hand was ever
active, and once again we have the impression that the effect of a direct
account may be somewhat stronger than its actual veracity.

In his commentary Bale follows objectives similar to those in *Oldcastle*.
He again attacks the persecutors, opposes their doctrines, and shows
that the events here, partly derived form the direct source and partly

narrated by himself, can be given scriptural parallels. An alleged thunderclap at Anne's execution is compared to the biblical storm at the crucifixion (sig. I3). The dispute over transubstantiation arising from Anne's rejection of it attracts particular attention (sigs. E1–E1ᵛ). At times Anne is made a mouthpiece for a direct exposition of the doctrines promulgated by Bale (sigs. B3–B5ᵛ). However, it has been noted that most of the language allegedly written by Anne in the parts devoted to her account is much simpler and indeed less abusive than the language of the commentary. While it is possible that this is a fictional activity by Bale, it does seem more likely that there is a measure of authenticity here, and one which Bale as an editor and maker of books was not unaware of. When Foxe came to recount the story of Anne in *Acts and Monuments*, he used her words as reported, without Bale's commentary.[17]

Bale made another contribution to Protestant hagiology by his manuscript translation into Latin of the *Examination of William Thorpe*, which he added to the *Fasciculi Zizaniorum*. It should be remembered, however, that Bale does not usually use the word "saint" for such notables. His observance of the death of Luther, *The True History of the Christian Departing of the Reverend Man, D. Martin Luther* (1546), a translation from Justus Jonas and others, is quiet in tone. Although it is a translation, the text shows a concern for quite minute circumstantial detail which emerges elsewhere, as we shall see in the *Vocation*. He gives a brief account which stresses that Luther experienced a quiet and peaceful death, adding funeral orations by Justus Jonas, Philip Melanchthon, and John Pomerane and a prayer by the Duke of Saxony. These draw attention to doctrinal aspects to which Bale was sympathetic, especially justification by faith, the avoidance of idolatry, and the direct use of scripture by the individual Christian. Melanchthon speaks of the direct access of the Christian to God without intermediary (sig. 16ᵛ).

The last work which may be considered as part of the new sainthood is the *Vocation*, Bale's autobiographical account of his appointment to the see of Ossory in Ireland in 1552–53. Even though the subject is Bale himself, the book includes little self-examination, nor indeed does it reveal much of Bale's personal feelings about his life during this period. To write about oneself drawing a parallel between one's own journeys and St. Paul's mission to the Gentiles may seem the height of vanity, but really the purpose is to witness thankfully the working of God's grace resulting in deliverance from enemies, and to cast obloquy on the Antichrist appearing in the form of papal abuses in the Irish Church. The latter, as Bale discovered and graphically describes—no doubt with little understatement—had held on to the old religion through the reigns of Henry VIII and Edward VI, and greeted the accession of Queen Mary with rejoicing (sig. C8). It ought perhaps to be added that Bale had found plenty to complain of in England, as his comments on the Rank Papist of Hampshire and on the Catholics in Cornwall indicate, but he made the most of what he found in Ireland. Doctrinally the work points to the true calling of Christian priests as against the falseness of the papists, the purity of the ancient British Church before the coming of St. Augustine, and the continuing presence of virtuous Christians up to the present time, especially Wyclif, Tyndale, and John Frith.

The *Vocation* falls into three parts. Initially, the doctrinal issues mentioned are elaborated, with some reference to Bale's historical perceptions of the ancient English kings and the mythology surrounding them (sigs. B1–B7ᵛ). The central and largest section is a detailed account of Bale's appointment to the bishopric by King Edward, his journey to Ireland, his attempt to bring forward Protestant practices which in turn aroused bitter hostility, his decision to flee, his adventures on the sea at the hands of a rapacious pirate who sought unsuccessfully to make a profit by selling him to the English authorities on two occasions, and his eventual deliverance to the Low Countries (sigs. B8–F2ᵛ). The last section is an address to the Church of England, now persecuted under Mary but enjoined by Bale to look for greater things precisely because of the persecution (sigs. F3–G1).

In the central narrative Bale chooses his opportunities to relate scandalous stories of the papist clergy, but the account is remarkably circumstantial and informative about the realistic details of the whole sequence of events. Some specific dates are given, and many individual names and places are specified, to the extent that one suspects he was writing from a diary. In his usual fashion he gives a transcript of the letter of his appointment, and at times he seems to be repeating his sermons verbatim. There is also a good measure of direct speech:

"What will ye gyve than," sayde the Captaine, "to be delivered into Flaunders, and our purser to be called [back] againe?"

I answered that I wolde gyve as his selfe wolde with reason and conscience require.

"If ye had tolde us so muche yester night," saide he, "this matter had bene at a point, and we by this tyme had bene in Zelande!"

(sig. E7ᵛ; punctuation and layout modernized)

The narrative itself is often clear and tense, as in:

> The next daye in the afternone behelde they two English shippes more
> whome they chaced all that night longe, and the next daye also till ten of
> the clocke; and one of them they toke by reason that his topsaile brake,
> and that was a shippe of Lynne. In this they had nothinge but apples, for
> he went for his loadinge. (sig. E5ᵛ)

In the second group of polemical works Bale responds to particular
circumstances and seeks to draw out his doctrinal objectives. During his
first exile he adopted the pseudonym John Harrison for *Yet a Course at the
Romish Foxe* (Zurich, 1543). His target was Bishop Bonner, whose pressure on a priest called William Tolwyn to recant earned Bale's scorn. He
called Bonner the Romish Foxe and perceived him as an agent of the
pope among the English Bishops. Bale follows his customary method of
commentary by giving Tolwyn's statement and interpolating his own
views. The latter stress the historical corruption of bishops, and their
treachery to the nation:

> the kynge thus doynge one thynge and the bysshoppes an other. (fol. 34ᵛ)

Bale brings out the familiar theme of the place of persecution in the life
of the true Christian:

> The trewe churche of Christ knowne . . . but by persecucyon for
> ryghtousnesse sake. (fol. 16)

and

> I knowe I schal be burned yf I maye be caught. (fol. 9)

He draws attention to other victims in Richard Mekyns, a 17–year-old
who was burned (fols. 24–24ᵛ), John Porter, and John Frith. He attributes Frith's execution in 1533 to Bishops Stokesley and Gardiner (fol. 57ᵛ).
He advocates the marriage of the clergy, including the bishops (fol. 70).
He accuses Bonner of setting up English Bibles in St. Paul's with a view
to catching reformers—"not purposynge anye christen erudycyon to the
peple, but as snares to catche them by" (fol. 93). His polemic even continues in the index to the volume where Bonner appears as 'an angell of
the bottomlesse pitt." Similarly, in *Vocation* Bale continues the castigation

of his enemies in the index: "Richarde Routhe—a lecherous Judas . . . Thomas Hothe, a wicked justice."

The attack "against the pompouse popyshe Byshoppes . . . and theyr fylthye father the great Antichrist" continued in *The Epistle Exhortatory* (1544) which appeared under the pseudonym Henry Stalbridge, and may have been a collaboration with William Turner. There is concern here for the ways in which the author(s) thought the bishops had misled monarchs historically, including King John, and they are alleged to have tried to make King Henry follow him by inducing him to be subservient to Rome after the Six Articles (fols. vii, ix^v–x^v). Henry is urged to reject the bishops and to dispossess them of their wealth (fols. xxi–xxiii^v). The true role of the bishops is described as "to instructe the multitude in the wayes of God, and to se that they were not beastlye ignoraunt in the holye scriptures" (fol. xxvii^v). There is a list of honest (Protestant) martyrs (fol. xiii), and the bishops are rebuked for their proceedings against players; no doubt these proceedings were a response by the bishops to Cromwell's use of plays (Bale's included) for polemical purposes in the previous decade:

> Non leave ye unvexed and untroubled. No, nott so moch as the pore mynstrels and players of interludes, but ye are doynge with them. So long as they played lyes and sange bawdye songes, blaspheminge God and corrupting mennes consciences never blamed them but were very well contented. (fols. xvi–xvi^v)

His parting shot to Gardiner is: "The Lorde sende yow herafter a more godly sprete or take ye sone hence" (fol. xxx^v).

In view of the severity of Bale's attacks upon particular bishops, and upon the misuse, as he saw it, of their office, it is ironic that he himself became a bishop in 1552 under King Edward. However, his tenure did not last long, and during his second exile, which followed, he returned to that attack by publishing an English translation of Stephen Gardiner's *De Vera Obedientia* (1553). Gardiner had been party to the negotiations for the divorce of King Henry VIII from Catherine and had published this work in 1536 in support of royal supremacy, a key policy in making the divorce possible. Gardiner became more and more conservative during the last part of Henry's reign, but he fell out of favor and retired to his see at Winchester. He was appointed Lord Chancellor by Queen Mary and became a leading figure in the restoration of the ways of the old religion. Bale saw that in drawing attention to Gardiner's change of approach he might damage Gardiner, and he exercised his editorial and translating skills to bring this about. His introduction notes changes in Gardiner's attitude to "mennes tradicions," and to the liturgy, and links him again with Bonner:

> and now even he with his blowboll bocherly brother Boner (turnyng lyke wethercockes, ersy versy, as the wynd bloweth) do . . . go about judaslye to repeale the just and right supreme power and authoriti incident bi Gods own word and lawe to the imperial crowne of England abusyng the quenes graces lenitie and most gentle nature. (sig. A4)

Shifting his line quickly, Bale also argues that by the original work Gardiner ("a scabbed Cuckow bird") had tried to make Mary a bastard (sig. A8). In the text itself Bale again interrupts with his own comments, endorsing Gardiner's earlier views where it suits him, especially over obedience to the sovereign and over the constancy of God's law (sigs. D5, G1). He adds his own views about clerical celibacy and the papist practices now returning, advocating the true church as an "olde plaine russet cote Jone of the countri" (sig. I7ᵛ).

Not long after this, in 1554, Bale apparently wrote *A Declaration of Edmund Bonner's Articles* in Basel (1561), though the work did not appear until after his return to London. In this work Bale's faith is shown positively at times:

> the heavenlye benefyte of remyssyon . . . [is] fullye attained by an earnest faythe in Goddes lyvely promises coupled with true repentance. (sig. Lvᵛ) Lyght is now come into the worlde. If we passe not for it we muste by oure own foly perysh in the darcknesse. (sig. Aiii)

But the abuse of Bonner, who had published 126 articles of examination, and of his episcopal colleagues continues. Bonner is "the blody biteshepe of London" (sig. Aii), and Bale also mentions "gagling Gardiner . . . and trifeling Tunstall." He again attacks the papist clergy, and he specifies the wrongs done, in his view, by Hildebrand (c. 1015–85) and Anselm (1033–1109). By this time Bale had worked out his attitude to the perversions of the faith in historical terms, and these views informed many of his works from the 1540s through to the 1560s. He again uses the technique of quoting the original target document and interpolating his commentary. The effect of this is to set up a kind of dialogue with his opponent, in which Bale has the last word. At

one point Bale repeats his attitude to the clergy in a form reminiscent of
King Johan: the clergy are a "shaven and disguised nacion . . . begynners
of sedicyon, sowers of tumulte" (sig. Hvii). The Latin service is, prover-
bially, "a blynde leadynge . . . of the blynde" (sig. Kii).

One of Bale's most outspoken works, *The Expostulation or Complaint
against the Blasphemyes of Frantic Papist of Hampshire* (London, 1552), seems
to have been an attempt to obtain preferment, and indeed it may have
been contributory to his elevation to the episcopacy in the same year. On
his return from Germany in 1548, he had to wait some time before he
obtained a living at Bishopstoke in Hampshire. This may have been
because he had antagonized Sir William Paget, the secretary of state, by a
recent mention of him in connection with the torturing of Anne Askew.[18]
At Bishopstoke he seems to have been part of the chaplaincy of the new
Protestant Bishop of Winchester, John Ponet. The *Expostulation* is dedicated to the Duke of Northumberland, and its main objective is to hang a
polemical attack against the old religion upon Bale's outrage toward a particular unnamed Hampshire cleric, and against the unreformed local practices of the clergy ("stought sturdy satellytes of Antichrist . . . chefely
within Hamshire," sig. Aiiᵛ). It looks a bit like a personal animus, because
the unidentified enemy had interfered in Bale's household as well as
encouraged papist practices. Bale accuses him of taking part in the persecution of Protestants: "with frothe yssuynge out on both sydes of hys
mouthe for anger" (sig. Ciiiᵛ), and he complains of a physical attack (sig.
Civ). There had also been an attempt to bring charges against Bale at the
Winchester Sessions (sig. Civ). It is in this context that Bale refers to a
planned performance of *Three Laws*. The papist reviled Bale's servant:

> calling hym a heretyke and knave because he had begonne to studie a
> parte in suche a Comedie as myghtely rebuked the abhomynacyons and
> fowle fylthie occupienges of the Bishopp of Rome. Moreover he requyred
> hym in hys own stought name to do a lewde massage whych was to call
> the compiler of that Comedie both heretike and knave, concludynge that
> it was a boke of most perniciouse heresie. (sig. Cii)

The theme of persecution thus appears clearly; there is "no Abel unles he
be vexed of some maliciouse Cain" (Aivᵛ).

One passage in the *The Frantic Papist* leads us on to a consideration of
verse in Bale's polemical work. Although it is printed as prose, the
rhythmical aspects of the following give a sense of how verse, strengthened by alliteration, might enhance the intensity of Bale's polemic:

> They bragge, they boast, they dreme, thei dote, thei fume, thei face, thei
> grunte, they grudge, they jangle, they jest, they mocke, they mowe, they
> scoffe, they scorne, they ruffle, they rage, wyth dagger and with fyste,
> and all to stoppe the swete blastes of the scriptures. (Aiii`<sup>v</sup>`)

All of Bale's extant plays are in verse, and there is no reason to suppose
that the many lost plays were not similar. (Prose is, after all, very rare in
the English drama before Lyly and Shakespeare.) He was clearly experienced in this respect and able to use many different forms. A discussion
of his dramatic verse appears below, but here we can consider the nondramatic aspects, which are not so prolific.

In *An Answer to a Papistical Exhortation* (1548), Bale prints and replies
in verse to a papist attack using dimeters and rime couée:

> Your fayth is so weake
> No treuth can ye speake
>   But hate all godly wayes.
> Ye robbe Christes flocke
> And geve them a mocke
>   In all your juglynge playes.[19]

His sections of commentary are supported by extra-metric biblical quotations, usually two in each stanza. He begins by insulting the poetic
powers of his opponent:

> Everye pylde pedlar
> Wyll be a medlar
> Though ther wyttes be drowsye
> And ther lernynge lowsye,
> Ther meters all mangye
> Rashe, rurall and grangye;
> Yet wyll they forwarde halte
> As manne mased in malte. (sig. A2)

This rapid and pithy versification may recall the so-called Skeltonics of
John Skelton's poetry.

The *Resurrection of the Mass* is dated 1554 from Strasbourg, but it has
been suggested that the date should be 1555, the work being a
response to the proclamation against seditious books of 1555.[20] The
attribution to Bale is probable (STC 13457) on the grounds that the
objects of attack are frequently his: Gardiner, auricular confession,

"smered shavelinges," the costume required for the Mass, celibacy, and purgatory. The poem is allegedly written for the comfort of Catholics, as the title-page claims, "newly set forth unto the greate hartes ease, joye and comforte of all Catholykes," and the resurrection would no doubt be the revival of the traditional Mass under Mary, a topic mentioned in the *Vocation*. It is a monologue spoken by the personified Mass addressed to Catholics, but the manipulation of meaning is apparent in the comment upon transubstantiation:

> And although ye bothe se, fele, and taste bred
> Yet muste ye nedes beleve the contrarie,
> For holy Churche hath full determined
> That it is Christes naturall bodye. (sig. Av)

The ironically and sarcastically inverted Protestant view is apparent:

> Of Christ and his holy Gospel
> Of true fayth, hope and charite
> I have nothing at all to tell
> For that dothe not belong to me. (sig. Aii)

There is a list of diseases the Mass can cure, and it may also help in acquiring spouses (sig. Aiii), and give relief from Purgatory (sig. Avii). It is perhaps in this work that Bale is closest to the rhetorical methods of *Three Laws*.

Two other works in verse attracted Bale's attention as an editor. *A Mystery of Iniquity* (Antwerp, 1545) quotes the verses of one Ponce Pantolabus. This is thought to have been John Huntington who in fact turned Protestant before Bale's edition of his poem appeared,[21] and who attacked the Protestants by relating a genealogy of heresy, showing, for example, that Mischief was the father of Wyclif:

> Wylfullnesse verilye
> Nygh cosyne to heresye
> Begate myschefe
> Father of Wyclefe
> Which ded bringe inne
> His grandfather synne. (fol. 8)

Bale offers his commentaries on the doctrine of the original after each section and substitutes his own doctrine. He expands especially upon

Wyclif and his supporters, including John Hus, and among contemporaries he defends his contemporaries—Martin Luther, Philip Melanchthon, Johannes Oecolampadius, Huldreich Zwingli, and John Frith. In speaking of the Antichrist he has a special role for:

> the four orders of fryeres which came last of all [and] are the tayle that covereth his arse which is now cut off in Englande and therfore he is become a curtall [docked horse]. (fol. 54)

In this work Bale also attacks the saints and the *Legenda Aurea* of Jacobus de Voragine, which was probably the most popular hagiography (fol. 60ᵛ). His sense of poetic decorum leads him to criticize the versification of the original on the basis that the number of syllables per line is not strictly matched:

> some of them daunse lyke great gyauntes and are eyght syllabes a pece . . . Some come doppynge after lyke lyttle hoppe on my thombes and are but four syllables. (fol. 46)

A year later in *Rhithmi Vetustissimi de Corrupte Ecclesiae Statu*, Bale published his edition in Latin of Walter Map's *Apocalipsis Goliae Pontificis*, which dates from about 200 years earlier. Bale was no doubt attracted because this poem attacks the corruption of the clergy, and he adds his own translation to point up the polemical effect. The poem contains a description of the Abbot feasting extravagantly with the brothers (sig. B2ᵛ).

Probably the earliest of Bale's more specifically doctrinal works was *A Christian Exhortation unto Customable Swearers* (1543). This work is a warning against blasphemy. The swearing of oaths seems to Bale to be quite unnecessary. Instead, one should use simple asseverations such as "yea, yea" and "no, no." The issues raised here are closely related to his contempt for the swearing of oaths which may not be kept, especially the monastic oath relating to chastity. The point is put sharply in the *Apology*:

> Who can vowe that hys heare shall not growe, nor his nayles increase and fulfyll it in effecte? No more can they do to lyve chaste onlesse the Lorde geve it, whyche he never doeth in causes unnecessary. (fol. 4)

In *Customable Swearers* Bale is again reacting against the papist clergy, especially over the making of vows and over celibacy. His criticism is so sharp that he claims that only Rome has priests, that Christ set up none (fol. cix^v); and that his opponent, the Rank Papist, is possessed by the devil (fol.xcvii^v). We can see here also his respect for St. Augustine of Hippo, an important influence upon Luther.[22] The rhetorical mode here draws upon imagery of a proverbial nature:

> In thys ye fare lyke the back [bat] or owle whyche seeth all in the darke and nothyng in the clere lyght. (fol. lvi)

He likens his opponent to the Catholic controversialist, Eckius: "lyke wyl to lyke as the devyl fyndeth out the colyar" (fol. xciii).

The *Image of Both Churches* and the *Acts of English Votaries* are the most ambitious part of Bale's doctrinal works during his first exile. They were not dependent upon external or topical circumstances as many of his other works were; instead, they seem to have been conceived as major contributions to the evolution of Protestant thought. The *Image* was probably begun when Bale went into exile in 1540, its main purpose being to rewrite history in terms of the Book of Revelation. It was first published in three parts at Antwerp in 1545 and was reprinted in London in 1548, 1550, 1560 and 1570. Copies were burned on Bonner's authority in 1546. *Votaries* drew heavily upon Bale's research as a Carmelite in the 1520s and was contrived to show "their unchaste practices and examples by all ages." It was probably being compiled for publication from about 1544. It first appeared at Antwerp in 1546, and was enlarged and reprinted in London in 1548, 1551, and 1560.

Bale's interpretation of history according to the book of Revelation owes much to the *Exegeseos in Sanctam divi Joanis Apocalypsim* (Basel, 1539) by Francis Lambert (1487–1530), whom he mentions in his list of sources and notes. This in turn depended upon the identification of the papacy as Antichrist by Joachim di Fiore (c. 1135–1202), who forecast, in an interview with King Richard II, the ascendancy of the Antichrist after 1260.[23] This view was followed by Wyclif and Luther, as Fairfield shows (1976, 68–89). Blatt points out (47) that there are many other references to the Antichrist before Bale, and she cites Tyndale, *The Parable of the Wicked Mammon* (1527), *The Answer to Sir Thomas More's Dialogue* (1531), and *The Obedience of a Christian Man* (1528). The coming of the Antichrist gave the lead for the idea of the opening of the seven seals in Revelation as seven ages of the history of the Church since Christ, with special significance for the year 666 (the

FIG. 1 THE SON OF MAN, REVELATION 1:16–17

FIG. 2 THE BINDING OF SATAN, REVELATION 20:1–2

The vocacyon
of Johā Bale to the
bishopꝛick of Ossoꝛie in Jre
lāde his persecuciōs in ꝑ̃ same/ꝛ
finall delyueraunce.

The English Chꝛistiā / The Jrishe Papist.

℣ God hath deliuered me from the snare of the
hunter/ꝛ frō ꝑ̃ noysome pestilēce.psal.xcj.
℣ Jf J must nedes reioyce/J wil reioyce
of myne infirmytees. ij. Coꝛ.xj.

FIG. 3   TITLE PAGE OF *Vocation*

coming of Theodoric as Archbishop of Canterbury), and for the release
of Satan from captivity in A.D. 1000. For this task Bale saw his role as
analogous to that of St. John of Patmos. He added much to the outline,
perhaps because he had accumulated a great quantity of historical
material, perhaps because the primacy of the Bible was essential to his
theology:

> The trewe Christen churche is alone governed by the preachynge of God's
> worde. (sig. aii)

Revelation is the most important book for him because it commends
righteousness and condemns heresy (sig. aii). Its authority outweighs
that of the chronicles:

> It is a full clerenes [clarification] to all the cronicles and moste notable
> hystories which hath bene writen sense Christes ascension. (sig. aiv^v)

In fact, Bale's work is a full commentary upon Revelation. The English
text is cited verse by verse, and each section is followed by Bale's exege-
sis. From a literary point of view he is carrying out a specific role as biblical exegetic here.

The title of *The Image of Both Churches* draws attention to the True and
False Churches which Bale saw as opposed to one another throughout
history, mirroring the opposition of Christ and Satan. The idea of an
image is supported by woodcuts which show the two forms—"The poore
persecuted churche of Christe or immaculate spowse of the lambe," and
"The proude paynted churche of the pope or synnfull Synagoge of
Sathan."[24] There is a distinct possibility that St. Augustine's *City of God*
was influential on Bale's division. This book described a division between
the *civitas dei* and the *civitas terrena*, the latter being interwoven with the
former.[25]

The seven periods of history are seen as periods of trial for the true
church, "to trye her as golde in the fornace" (sig. Ovi^v). This appears
to be a distinct departure from the earlier divisions of history into
three periods (Nature, Moses and Christ) in *Three Laws*, and into
seven (from Adam to Christ) in *God's Promises*. Bale elaborated the
detail of the seven ages considerably, but in broad outline the seven
were as follows:

The **First** Age followed the revelation of the Holy Spirit at Pentecost
and was developed by the apostles (sig. Ovii^v).

The **Second** Age began with the attacks upon the Church by the Roman emperors, especially Diocletian, but at this time the popes and fathers followed the truth (sig. Ovii^v).

The **Third** Age followed the establishment of the Church under Constantine, though it contended with disputes and heresies (sigs. Pi–Pii).

The **Fourth** Age began the period of papal tyranny in 607 with the proclamation of Boniface III as the universal bishop. At this point superstitions developed in the form of censing, bell-ringing, holy water, and processions. This was also the time of the mission of St Augustine to Canterbury, bringing corrupt ways, and of the rise of Islam (sigs. Pii^v–Piii^v).[26]

The **Fifth** Age was marked by the release of Satan from captivity, and this meant that he was now able to come out into the world and further the persecution of true Christians, as in the cases of the Waldensians and the Albigensians. It was a time of the growth of religious orders, which Bale characterized as the age of locusts (sigs. Pvi^v–Qi^v).

The **Sixth Age** contained the revival of the Gospel in the time of Wyclif, but it also brought worse attacks upon the faithful (sigs. Rii–Riii).

The **Seventh** Age, beginning with the Reformation, marked the coming of the millenium on earth, anticipating the Second Coming (sigs. Sv^v–Svi^v).

There is little continuous writing in *Image* and the items of faith and belief are presented in short passages, for Bale sees the original as requiring a commentary. Thus the White Horse of the Apocalypse is seen as the true minister and perfect preacher of the apostles' doctrine (sig. Ee^v). On the loosing of Satan, Bale says, "Afore that Sathan was thus at lyberte he remayned secrete in the hearts of men. Now he is abrode in theyr outwarde ceremonyes and rytes, readye to be seane of all the world," (sig. Ggvi). On the communion he asserts his belief: "the holy supper of the Lord . . . is no newe sacrifice to be made, but onely a fayth-full remembraunce to be taught of that ful and perfect sacrifice that he made once for all" (sig. Hhvi^v). Even the destruction of Jerusalem by Vespasian and Titus is seen as the will of Christ:

> utterlye to destroy that priesthode because we should put no trust in such thynges, nor yet be addict or bounde to places. (sig. 2, Ooii)

The popularity of *Votaries* was probably due in part to its somewhat sensational anecdotes about sexual activities in the monastic orders. The following escapade is typical:

Saynt Edwyne, kynge of Northumberlande gave unto Saynt Paulinus the
archebyshop of Yorke his yonge daughter Eanfleda . . . as she was baptysed in the yeare of our Lord 626 that he shuld make her an unholye
nonne. And the daye after the sayd Edwyne was slayne he toke with hym
both the doghter and mother, and so fled with them unto Rochester in
Kent by water, never returnynge thydre again. (sig. D7ᵛ)

Bale gives Capgrave as his authority for this tale.

Votaries was intended to be in four parts, each covering a period of
English Church history: from the beginnings when Joseph of Arimathea
first brought apostolic Christianity to Britain up to A.D. 1000; from
1000 to the time of King John; from King John to King Henry IV; and
from then to the present (sig. T7ᵛ). Bale managed to complete only the
first two parts. Although the work was conceived at the same time as
Image, it does not follow the seven-period structure described there. One
explanation for this is that Bale's theories were flexible according to
immediate needs; but another may lie in his sense that England was a
specially blessed place where the papal contamination arrived late, and
was, he thankfully held, expelled early—in 1533.

The essential thesis of Bale's view of history is that there are two
divisions in the godhead: one governs and the other teaches. This
extended through Adam, Noah, Moses, and Christ; but the Votaries,
following the Antichrist, have destroyed these (sigs. A3–A6). He
mentions that the evidence has been collected out of the legends of
the Votaries themselves, an oblique reference to his own Carmelite
journeys and collections. He refers also on several occasions to John
Capgrave's *Catalogus sanctorum Angliae*. In his letter of 30 July 1560 to
Archbishop Parker this is identified as the *Nova Legenda Angliae*,
which was printed by Wynkyn de Worde in 1516.[27] Bale apparently
lost a manuscript of this work in Ireland, as it is number 43 on his list
of lost works.

Closely associated with the false holiness of saints was the doctrine of
celibacy. Against the latter Bale defended marriage, saying it was insti-
tuted in Paradise and followed by the marriage of the ancient priesthood.
Elsewhere he condemned virginity without fruit as deserving no merit
(*Apology*, fol. xcixᵛ). The domination of the papacy in the seventh century
led to the doctrine that the marriage of priests was fornication after 710
(*Votaries*, sig. H1). In England it was Dunstan who first forced men and
women to swear chastity, and Bale gives an extensive treatment of him
as one who prepared the way for the release of Satan. At Dunstan's

death in 987 there were signs of blood. A further omen occurred in 1012 when the Danes sacked Canterbury.

Much of Part Two of *Votaries* is concerned with the struggle between the papacy and kings and emperors. The shorter historical period gives Bale scope for much detail against his chosen enemies. He questions the holiness of Edward the Confessor and his wife Edith, and attacks Peter Lombard whose *Sentences* were central to medieval theology and education. He makes it clear that the identification of the Antichrist with the pope can also be paralleled in what might be termed the local circumstances of English history. This is found in Anselm, "whych was the great Pope or Antichrist of Englande" (*Votaries*, II, Iv); according to Bale he banished clerical marriage. Anselm's evil nature is linked with that of Langfranc (d. 1089) by the appearance of stars to express divine displeasure (sigs. G7^v–G8). Bale is particularly aggressive about St. Thomas à Becket, criticizing him for his lascivious youth and his defense of priests against the law of the land (sig. Q1^v).

Two other short works show Bale working on particular aspects of doctrine. The interesting feature is that they are both written in dialogue form. The more serious and solemn is *A Dialogue or Communication to be had at table between two children* (1549). The title page adds that it was written for Bale's two young sons, John and Paul. The tone of this work is sober and restrained, the elder brother taking the lead in explaining the importance of faith directed by the New Testament. Men's traditions are condemned, but the emphasis is upon reasonable persuasion. The *Dialogue between Two Neighbours* (1554) is a more satirical affair in which Oliver, a professor of (believer in) the Gospel, seeks to instruct Nicholas, "noseled in blind superstition." Nicholas believes in transubstantiation and he refers to the authority of his priest, Sir John, over images and pilgrimages. Oliver is interested in making his points by ridicule:

> what apes play made thei of it in great Cathedral churches and abbayes . . .
> [the priest] stood mum and played Judas that betrayed the Mayster
> (Diii^v–Div)

To sum up Bale's method in these works we need to take account of his varied stances as an author. The accumulation of data acquired from his studies, preserved in the form of notes, is fundamental to his method. His frequent interest in translation is a significant feature of his expository role. Besides the translations of *De Vera Obedientia*, *William Thorpe*, and *The True History of Luther*, he also worked on *A Compendious Letter of*

John Pomerane, and on the *De Morte* of Baptista Mantuanus (STC 22992). This last was a fourteenth-century poet he much admired, a Carmelite, who "smelled out more abuses in the Romysh churche then in those dayes he durst well utter" (sig. Aii). Bale says that his translation here is made "paraphrastically," which apparently means that it is in prose and contains Bale's expansion and commentary within it. Nevertheless, his version reflects some of the imagery of the original: sickness as the warrior of death (sig. C2ᵛ), and "The mynde sent into this corruptible bodi entereth as doth a maier into a citie" (sig. B2).

Associated with Bale's work as translator is his role of commentator. He wrote an introduction to *A Godly Meditation of the Christian Soul* (1548), which, as the title page indicates, was originally written by Margaret of Navarre and translated by Princess Elizabeth at the age of 14. In his conclusion Bale follows up a theme mentioned in both parts of *Anne Askew*, the virtue of Christian women. He gives a list of scriptural quotations detailing the lives of good women (sig. E6ᵛ). Besides praising Elizabeth for her learning, he refers to Askew, and, using the traditional pre-Shakespearean version of the King Lear story, comments that Cordilla comforted Leyer "and restored hym agayne to hys princely honoure and reigned alone after hys deathe" (sig. F2ᵛ). Bale's role as commentator allows him to adduce additional information to the text he is editing and also allows him to intervene in the text in various ways, especially by interpolated commentary and by marginal annotation, which may be either purely factual or exclamatory. Where he is working over an existing text, this makes his intervention very pointed. It has the effect of setting up a kind of dialogue with his chosen text, or indeed with the author behind the text. Sometimes his tone is prophetic, but more often it is aggressive and sometimes it is insulting. From time to time he addresses the reader, who he assumes is a pious Christian.

He is quick to introduce contemporary anecdotes into his discussions, as with the account of his wife Dorothy's visit to Norwich in 1545 which he interpolates into *Votaries*, where the justice and the mayor interrogated her "grennyng upon her lyke termagauntes in a playe" (sig. O4). He seems interested in demotic speech and in bringing the language of conversation and dialogue into his prose works. This gives rise to many colorful expressions and to the use of proverbs. Expressions like "Whan the wylye foxe fawneth, beware your chyckens" (*Romish Fox*, fol. 44) and "Moche water cometh by the mylle (they saye) that the miller taketh not in" (*Mystery of Iniquity*, fol. 68) fit in with his image as a bluff straight-speaking Englishman, who avoids the unnecessary sophistication associated with the foreign papists. One may doubt, however, whether his expression is always so innocent and plain as he advocates in *A Mystery of Iniquity*: "He that doth speake the thynge that is true and certayne and without false colours doth utter it in wordes playne is moche better occypyed" (fol. 60ᵛ).

We may also note the absence of classical reference in his works, though there are indications that he had access to some ancient writers. The reason for his suspicion may well be his association of Aristotle with medieval scholasticism. On St. Augustine's mission to Canterbury he comments: "Wel armed were they with Aristotle's artylery, as with logycke, philosophy, and other craftye scyences, but of the sacred scryptures they knew little or nothyng" (*Votaries*, sig. D5). However, his position is complex because of his ambivalent attitude toward contemporary humanism. He recognized and acknowledged the value of the scholarship of Erasmus, especially over his interpretation of the works of St. Augustine of Hippo (*Apology*, fol.xxxvii ᵛ). Some significant doctrinal parallels can be found between Bale's views and those of Erasmus in the *Enchiridion Militis Christiani*.[28] Like Bale, Erasmus repudiated specialist and elitist Latin and scholastic philosophy; he produced a critique of monasticism; and he saw chastity and marriage as indistinguishable, and advocated an unsacramental inner religion. However, Bale could not approve humanists who remained largely within the Catholic church.

Sometimes we can also hear the minatory or accusatory tones of the preacher, which Bale regarded as fundamental to his role as a priest and indeed as a bishop. This may be reflected in the rhythmic aspects of his language, with alliteration, repetition, and rhyme all appearing in his prose from time to time. Such is his sense of the importance of relaying the word of God that he does not hesitate to compare his utterances to those of St. Paul and to those of St. John of Patmos. This is no doubt an aspect of his role as witness, which he regarded as essential, especially in a time of persecution such as that he endured during his two exiles.

Bale's position as an exile, and perhaps the need to avoid the risk of being captured and executed—as Tyndale was at Brussels in 1536—led him to adopt pseudonyms, and to provide false dates and places of publication. Besides the pseudonyms "Henry Stalbridge," "Hugh Hilarie," and "John Harrison," which have already been noted, and which he adopted to disguise his own identity, some of his works were allegedly printed at the press of Michael Wood, a name designed to cover the identity of his printers A. Goinus and John Day.[29] These devices show him as adept in propaganda.

Although some of the works discussed in this chapter were written after Bale's second exile, which began in 1553, it is clear that the bulk of them originated during the years 1540–48. The circumstances of the second exile were different from those of the first, in that a greater variety of Protestant views was represented in it. Moreover, Bale was older and may have been less keen to indulge in the short-term tactics of many of his minor works. But as we shall see in the chapter on his bibliographical writings, many of the preoccupations of the earlier polemics were preserved in the framework of the *Summarium* as it became expanded into the *Catalogus*. The latter was the principal fruit of the second exile, and it included in the expanded biographies and bibliographies a great deal of controversial material. The additions to *Catalogus* about the papacy were so extensive that Bale published them again as a separate work, *Acta Romanorum Pontificum* (1558). Perhaps because he was interested in reaching a readership of international scholars, especially in Germany, all these works too were in Latin.

Chapter Three
Literary History and Bibliography

In this chapter we shall turn to a miscellaneous group of works by Bale which, in general terms, reflects his interest in literary and historical matters. The emphasis here will be less upon controversy for the most part, though inevitably with Bale the orientation of the great majority of his works is determined by the theological objectives discussed in chapter 2. Indeed it is probably correct to say that matters of belief are at the heart of all Bale's works, and even the most scrupulous of his bibliographical activities is likely to have a justification deriving from them.

Manuscripts

Bale's manuscripts are likely to remain the concern of specialists rather than the general reader. As they will probably never be published in full, it is necessary to give some account of them here, including the objectives Bale set for himself in compiling them and some consideration of the contents. A survey of many examples of Bale's handwriting has indicated that they fall into five distinctive types. The most distinctive is that which he adopted in the early 1540s which is characterized by a long *r* and a tick over the letter *u/v*. He may have been influenced by the need to meet the needs of German printing houses which he was using at the time, but it is interesting that Luther's hand had a similar tick over *u/v*; thus the shift may have been ideological. This change in handwriting is very useful in dating Bale's manuscripts, and indeed in determining when revisions were made.[1]

The manuscripts which survive are chiefly working documents.[2] In later times many of them have been bound up in several compendia which contain work from different periods of Bale's working life, not necessarily in chronological order. He was in the habit of working over his material, adding notes, and changing details. Apart from the manuscript of *King Johan*, the special characteristics of which will be discussed in some detail in chapter 5, none of the extant manuscripts were meant for publication, and we have no holograph versions of any of the works that were actually printed, either plays or literary history.

On the whole, the notebooks that survive appear to be haphazard
accumulations of detail, built up rather unsystematically. The one exception to this is the Bodleian manuscript *MS Selden Supra 64* which was
given the title *Index Britanniae Scriptorum* by its editors when it was published in 1902.[3] This is thought to have been accumulated over the period 1548–57, when Bale was visiting many libraries and reviewing other
collections of books in preparation for the *Catalogus*. It is likely to have
traveled with him through his Irish journeys and into the second exile,
though the bulk of it would have been prepared before he left for Ireland
in 1552. As it happens his work on this manscript sheds no direct light
on how Bale went about organizing either the copy for the *Summarium* or
that for the *Catalogus*—endeavors which must have involved quite different transcription activities. The items in the index are listed alphabetically by Christian name of author, the notebook having been laid out in
advance in anticipation of the need under individual letters. The main
purpose is to make a comprehensive catalog of all known British
authors, giving titles and incipits, and showing either where Bale found
each book or what authorities he had used. This information about locations is bound to be very influential historically since it tells us so much
about the distribution of books and their subject matter. The survey has
implications for the provinces as well as for London. Bale visited many
libraries personally, especially colleges at Oxford (578) and Cambridge
(577), and many libraries in monastic houses, such as the one at
Norwich (578). He also visited royal libraries (577). His sources of information were medieval catalogs, and references embedded in medieval
texts generally. He acquired details from individual owners (over 100 are
listed by the editors on xix–xxxv), collectors, antiquaries, stationers, and
booksellers.

One characteristic of these notes, which has been observed by a number of critics, is that Bale seems to have collected this information in an
objective manner without making theological judgments about the people concerned. Only when he put the information into the *Catalogus* did
Bale add his customary and distinctive Protestant bias. A further indication of his method of working is that the *Index* lists each of Chaucer's
Canterbury Tales by name (75–6), whereas the *Catalogus* merely refers to
the Prologue, 24 tales, and the spurious Ploughman's Tale.

One manuscript already referred to in the previous chapters has a
unique place in his work in that it is a response to a particular circumstance, Bale's imprisonment at Greenwich in 1537.[4] However, it is difficult to assess the significance of *The Answer of John Bale, priest, unto certain*

articles unjustly gathered upon his preaching because we do not have the articles concerned, which must have contained allegations against Bale that originated from among his parishioners. The context of Bale's *Answer* is the rather delicate state of affairs after the publication of the King's Book, when there was great danger for people who went too far toward Protestant beliefs in defiance of the King's conservatism as it was now expressed. In this document Bale is arguing vigorously against various heresies that were supposedly embodied in his preaching. His emphasis is upon clarifying the things necessary for salvation, upon the true spiritual life which recognized the marriage of Christ to the soul, and upon the inner goodness which is more important than ceremonies. He gives a few insights into his own life including recognizing that he had once been a friar but now rejoiced in the change, as Paul had rejoiced in being no longer a Pharisee, and that he had written a play about the Harrowing of Hell which probably showed the struggle between Christ and the devils: "Yet can we not justlye suppose that he fawght vyolentlye with the devyls for the sowles of the faythfull sort."

As there is no reference to a play on this theme in any of Bale's lists, it seems likely that this play is another which he disowned after his conversion. He speaks vigorously against the parish gossiping that went on, in a passage in favor of the Catholic allegiance of the Pilgrimage of Grace and against Cromwell. As is so often the case, he is insistent upon attacking the worship of Mary and the saints and the ways in which he thought the papacy had falsely and avariciously promoted them. The right understanding of sainthood is fundamental to Bale's belief: "But all thei whych departed hens in fayth and testymonye of the wurde of God wer sayntes most lawfully canonysed or auctorysed in the blood of Crist."

Most of the rest of Bale's surviving manuscripts contain work collected before his conversion. Indeed in his lists of his works he tends to itemize the manuscripts as either *Collectiones Germanicae* or *Collectiones Gallicae*, suggesting that they were centered primarily upon his early journeys. However, the manuscripts, as noted above, are complex documents, and they are chiefly collections of items relating to his work within the Carmelite order. Virtually the whole of these works is in Latin, perhaps initially because Bale regarded this part of his work as relating to ecclesiastical history and later because Latin gave him access to an international Protestant readership.

We may here briefly describe three of these collections. Bodleian *MS Selden Supra 72* comprises a section of scribal exercises in which Bale seems to have set a pattern and others imitated it, subject to his correction. This section may have been part of his work as a teacher of novices at Cambridge. In another distinct section of the same manuscript, there is a list of Carmelite priors general which was probably composed by 1523. Elsewhere there are three Carmelite tracts that are not in Bale's hand, but do show his corrections.

Bodleian *MS Selden Supra 73* contains extensive notes on the history of Bale's order. This manuscript was probably collected from the Low Countries, where he visited Carmelite houses before 1523, though there are some later minor modifications.

Bale notes in *MS Harley 1819* that it contains material collected during his journey to France in 1527, which indicates it probably corresponds to the *Collectiones Gallicae* listed in the *Catalogus*. Among the items included are a life of St. Anne and several poems in Latin by Bale himself. The orthodox tone of these may well be noted from the antiphon to the Virgin, "Ave florens flos carmeli," which was written at Hitchin in 1526 (fols. 87^v-88; already referred to in chapter 1). The poem entitled "Votum balei ad beatam Johannam virginem" ("Bale's Prayer to the blessed virgin Joanna," fol. 144^v) celebrates Joanna's upbringing in the city of Toulouse, where the poem was composed in 1527. There are also two epitaphs by Bale in this manuscript.[5]

Two more extensive manuscripts show distinct signs of the changes in Bale's outlook, although in both cases a good deal of the material is firmly based in his Carmelite years. Bodleian *MS Selden Supra 41* consists of five different notebooks. The first comes close to being a literary anthology of Carmelite works, reflecting Bale's interest in poetry. Most of the poems are by others, notably by Baptista Mantuanus (1448–1516), who was prior of the order and whose *De Morte* Bale translated in 1551. The attractions seem to have been that Baptista exposed some corrupt practices within the order and that he offered a pattern for devotion. Many of the poems are unattributed, but a few short distichon are labeled as Bale's own. There are lives of Carmelite saints, a dialogue by Jan van Hildesheim on the order (a contemporary form of expression which Bale was to develop further after his conversion in a quasi dramatic mode), poems by the Carmelite Laurentius, and catalogs of priors general and of members who obtained the degree of doctor of divinity (D.D.) at Paris. The most important section, which Bale referred to as his *Fasciculus Carmelitorum*, is a history of the order, which was compiled between 1527 and 1533, with additions up to 1540, the year he went into exile. This section also shows a shift in attitudes, in that Bale becomes more critical of individual members. Although this section may shed some light on Bale's views, the whole work has considerable value because of the details it gives about the work of the order and because of the attitudes embodied in it. Bale puts emphasis upon its special devotion to the Virgin and upon its literary aspirations. In the Protestant part, Bale inserts a brief notice of his own life and works. This is the first of four extant versions of Bale's autobiography, as discussed in chapter one above. We should also note that, though it is brief, this section of the manuscript begins to foreshadow the biographical and bibliographical patterns of the *Summarium* and the *Catalogus*.

The British Library *MS Harley 3838* has three parts. The first, entitled *Anglorum Heliades* (fols. 3–112), is undoubtedly Bale's composition, being a history of the English Carmelites. Dedicated to John Leland, who had requested it, it is written in the hand of a scribe other than Bale, though his autograph corrections are to be found in it—for example, in the incipits to the plays in his personal bibliography.[6] The work contains an outline of the history of the Carmelites in England, which is followed by a collection of biographies of English Carmelites, together with lists of their works. The date is given as 1536, by which time Bale had converted. However, there are some items that must date from 1538 and some that date perhaps as late as 1540, giving the manuscript a somewhat fluid point of origin.

The other two parts of *MS Harley 3838* were probably written at different times, although they may have been intended to be complementary, making up a history of the Carmelites. It looks as though Bale first wrote the section from the twelfth century to about 1530, entitled *De Preclaris Ordinis Carmeli Scriptoribus ac Theologis Cathologus* (fols. 156–249), and then, in the *Perpaucorum Carmeli Scriptorum . . . Cathologus* (fols. 118–55) dealt with the mythical origins of the order from Elijah to Bertholdus, the first General Master of the order. This division is polemical, in that Bale sees the earlier period as devoid of the culpable and depraved practices of medieval Catholicism, especially in regard to such matters as vows of celibacy and clerical marriage. However, as Bale's aggressive comments on these practices are concentrated in the section dealing with the earlier history, it may be concluded that this part was written after his conversion. In spite of his attack upon the order in various places, here there is no doubt that Bale's accumulated information is invaluable in providing data on the history of the Carmelites.

The last manuscript that needs to be mentioned here was not originally by Bale at all. Bodleian *MS e Musaeo 86* is thought to have been in the Carmelite library in Norwich, and the collection is known as the *Fasciculi Zizaniorum*. Bale may have acquired it in 1538 and taken it into exile with him in 1540.[7] It is a collection of documents concerned with the activities of Wyclif and some of his followers, and sets out a considerable amount of Wycliffite doctrine in the exchanges between the Wycliffites and their Carmelite examiners. Even though the parts of this manuscript must have come from many different sources, the whole document appears to be the work of one scribe. It was intensively worked over by Bale as he sought to correct it and to extract from it significant aspects of Wycliffite doctrine and history as he saw it. At the beginning he seems to have given the volume his own title: *The Wars of Wycleff (Bella Vuicleui)*, and he writes on the same page, "The battayle of Johan Wycleffe and serten other c'sten [christen] souldyarys agaynst the synagoge of Sathan or malygnaunt cherche of the romyshe papa" (fol. 1ᵛ). His interpolations at the beginning contain a comment on Wyclif's views on transubstantiation in which Bale aligns him more closely with the views held by Oecolampadius and Zwingli than with those of Luther (fol. 1ᵛ). Bale makes one direct contribution in his translation into Latin of the *Examination of William Thorpe* (fols. 98ᵛ–103ᵛ). He also adds marginal notes such as "mendacius" (liar, fol. 63ᵛ), and "fabricant" (they are making this up, fol. 43ᵛ). The documents are especially strong in that they present a process of witnessing what went on—in a scriptural sense. There is a section of testimonies on behalf of Wyclif from various authors, including praise from Tyndale and Frith (fol. 149). However, some of the items Bale added are objective—such as a considerable number of dates, and three indexes to sections of the manuscript. All in all, we have the impression that Bale became very familiar with this volume, and that he inserted things into it which arose from a number of different considerations.

In the *Summarium* and the *Catalogus* Bale set out to accumulate and present a large amount of historical and bibliographical data. In some ways he had specific objectives related to his own particular time and circumstances. Clearly, however, and indeed by his own admission, he used methods employed by other writers before him in analogous collections. He seems to have had contrary impulses. While there is no doubt about his conversion and the extent of his conviction about Protestant ways of thinking, the Carmelite tradition was a distinctly literary one. Bale was sensitive to this circumstance, as his early compilations before his conversion suggest. Even though his Protestant outlook manifested itself in an urgent need to rewrite history and to vilify opposing views, Bale retained throughout his life a conscientious and meticulous attention to detail. As a result, much invaluable information was stored in his works, and some of it was about people whose position or opinions were anathema to him.

The tradition in which Bale chose to operate goes back to the primitive church, and it was rejuvenated with the invention of printing in the fifteenth century. The work of St. Jerome and the additions by Gennadius in the fifth century had recorded briefly the lives of illustrious Christians, with a view to upholding the faith.[8] The tradition actually starts with the lives of the apostles, especially St. Peter. There are one hundred lives in this collection, and Gennadius himself appears as the last—a device imitated by Bale in both his collections. The tradition was followed by Johan Tritenheim (Tritemius) in *De Scriptoribus Ecclesiasticis*, which was first printed at Basel in 1494 and reprinted at Paris in 1512. This work has a format for each biographical entry very similar to Bale's, with an introductory paragraph or so, followed by a list of works, with incipits. Bale had already used this structure in his early manuscript collection *Perpaucorum Carmeli Scriptorum*, which was written at the behest of John Leland in 1536.[9] The ideology and the people chosen by Tritenheim do not correspond to those in Bale's compilation. In some cases, as with the entry for Nicolaus de Lyra, Bale does seem to have followed Tritenheim's content as well as his method, though not the actual wording. Moreover Tritenheim's work is Catholic in orientation. Bale sometimes uses information from Tritenheim, but he adds a great deal, and much of what he adds is not complimentary to the subjects.

Bale's list of his lost works shows that he had accumulated a collection of authors in this genre. He claims to have had copies of Isidore's *De Ortu et Obitu Sanctorum Patrum* and *De Viris Illustribus*, of St. Jerome's *De Viris Illustribus*, and of a work of the same name by Gennadius (these two are probably interrelated, and the Gennadius is presumably a manuscript rather than an incunabulum), together with three tracts by Arnold Bostius also called *De Viris Illustribus*, and another of the same name by Laurentius Burellus, and still another by Johannes Trissa. Of Tritenheim he had a book "by the same title, with his own additions." He also had a "very old Catalogue of writers and learned men by an unknown author."[10] If we consider his notes about authorities used, and the observations made here about similarities of words and methodology, it is clear that these writers were the literary context for Bale's collections.

With Conrad Gesner (1516–65) we come closer to Bale's time and circumstances. Gesner and Bale corresponded, and Bale dedicated part of the *Catalogus* to Gesner. Gesner also was a Protestant, and one who shared Bale's anxiety about the loss of many manuscripts and books at the time of the Reformation. His *Bibliotheca Universalis* (Zurich, 1545) includes many individuals used by Bale, though he naturally gives much more space to the classical world to accord with his title: the article on Aristotle runs to 18 pages and contains quotations from the writings as well as listing them. Similarly, there is an extensive entry for Erasmus. In comparison with Tritenheim, Gesner adds much new material and fills in some of the incipits which had been left blank. His entries include extensive quotations from the authors treated. He departs from precedents by using alphabetical order. Bale, more deliberately but not exclusively concerned with the British tradition, which he was content to interpret somewhat loosely, and also impelled by his own reading of the mythical and specifically British past, makes his own selection of writers, although a number of writers are common to both authors. As Gesner's work is slightly earlier than Bale's, it seems certain that Bale would have known about it, but it is also probable that the two mutually encouraged one another, and that their independent preoccupations helped to characterize their work differently. Both continued to work in the genre for a considerable number of years.

Bale's work is, however, influenced by a slightly different precedent in Robert Barnes's *Vitae Romanorum Pontificum*, which contains a letter to Henry VIII dated 10 September 1535. The work was published at Wittenburg in that year and was partially translated by Luther in 1536. Bale's work shows a much firmer handling of biographical material on ideological grounds. Barnes, who was a colleague of Bale's at Cambridge, as we have noted, and who played a significant part in the evolution and dissemination of Protestant ideas until his execution in 1540, may have been aware of the tradition discussed here, but he does not pay close attention to its method. He does give short biographies, but his listing of works is spasmodic. However, the Protestant interpretation of history does inform his selection and treatment of individuals, and there is plenty of polemical comment on the individuals studied. Notably we find parallels with Bale's handling of such characters as Sylvester II and Stephen VI. It was Stephen VI who caused the exhumation of Formosus, a subject that was used by Bale several times in separate works. Most of Bale's closer borrowings from Barnes actually find their place in the antipapal historical narratives which Bale inserted into the *Catalogus* between the biographies, as appendices. They eventually reappeared in his *Acta Romanorum Pontificum*, whose title seems to recall that of Barnes.

Bale and Leland

Another influence that shaped Bale's bibliographical and biographical objectives must have been John Leland. We have seen that during the 1530s Bale had worked for Leland and prepared *Anglorum Heliades* at his prompting. By the time the *Summarium* appeared in 1548, Leland was probably in failing mental health. As King's Antiquary he had collected a great deal of historical information. Although Bale saw the *Summarium* as an interim measure pending the publication of Leland's work, it now became clear that Leland was too ill to bring out the work as he planned. After his return from exile in 1548, Bale gained access to some of Leland's work through the medium of Sir John Cheke, who had become Leland's executor.[11] This apparently prompted Bale to enlarge his research. He copied out his own epitome of Leland's *De Scriptoribus Britannicis*. Since Bale refers to himself as bishop of Ossory at the beginning of this manuscript, it must have been copied in or after 1552.[12] Bale added his own notes to Leland's work, and some of it was incorporated into both the *Catalogus* and the *Acta Romanorum Pontificum*. Bale's comments on Leland at this point show that he was somewhat uneasy about Leland's theological position. He observes that "many things are treated here without discrimination about doctrines or the investigation of the spirit, and evil things are accepted as though they were holy."[13]

Bale's edition of *The Laborious Journey and Search of John Leland for England's Antiquities* appeared in 1549 and was dedicated to Edward VI. It was a revival of a work given as a New Year's gift to Henry VIII. The form of the work is familiar from Bale's other editorial activities: he prints Leland's text with his own interpolations. Some of these are polemic, as for instance when he blames the papists for locking "up the gates of knowledge from them that affectuously seketh it to the glorye of God" (sig. C4ᵛ). He also adds detail to Leland's list of authorities (sigs. D1ᵛ–D2); this part of the work actually reveals the line of scholars writing literary biography originating with Jerome and Isidore, as noted above. He discusses Leland's objective in the light of work by Strabo, Pliny, and Erasmus. He has much praise for Leland in the Introduction as well as in the commentary , "For undoubted he was in these matters wonderfull and peerlesse" (sig. B5).[14] If Leland had not traveled, Bale thinks, the truth of the Bible would have been lost, and he also praises Leland for saving many old and authentic chronicles. The latter is an expression of the patriotic element in Bale's work on Leland's collections. He notes especially that the lack of knowledge of what is to be found in the chronicles had led to distortion and error in the chronicles of Harding, Caxton, Fabian, and Polydore Vergil. Translation would be an important way of supporting truth, and Bale was also interested in the publication of Anglo-Saxon and medieval texts.

Bale is most graphic in his outrage over the destruction of libraries:

> A great nombre of them whych purchased those superstycyouse mansyons [i.e., the monasteries and their libraries] reserved of those lybrarye bokes some to serve theyr jakes, some to scoure theyr candelstyckes, and some to rubbe theyr bootes. Some they solde to the grossers and sope sellers, and some they sent over see to the bokebynders, not in small nombre, but at tymes whole shyppes full, to the wonderynge of foren nacyons. (sig. B1)

> I have bene also at Norwyche, oure seconde cytie of name, and there all the library monumentes are turned to the use of their grosers, candel-makers, sope sellers and other worldly occupyers. (sigs. G3–G3ᵛ)

It is clear that Bale made contact at this time with printers and book-sellers as part of his search. He describes in some detail his own journeys since his return from Germany (sig. G2). He had visited certain places in Norfolk and Suffolk and would have extended his search more exten-sively "through out the whole realm yf I had bene able to have borne the charges, as I am not" (sig. G3ᵛ). His itinerary may be confirmed by the annotations in the *Index* about where manuscripts were found. Part of the program he envisages involves sponsorship by merchants, and he regrets that there had not been in every shire "but one solempne lybrary" (sig. B1). Near the end of the work he mentions the *Summarium* as sharing some of Leland's intentions, and he invites his readers to sub-mit further names for inclusion. At this point he also explains his plans for expanding his own bibliographical work.

The *Summarium* and the *Catalogus*

We must now consider the *Summarium* and the *Catalogus*, and describe the relationship between them. As we have seen, the *Summarium* as a book was generated during the first exile, from material Bale had been collect-ing for a number of years, and at a time when Bale was deeply involved in writing his shorter polemical tracts as well as creating his two major works of theological history, the *Image* and *Votaries*. The *Summarium* may perhaps be slightly less aggressively polemical than the *Catalogus*, but Bale makes it clear at the end, in the Peroratio, that he sees the centuries (i.e, hundreds) of writers as a rough parallel with the apocalyptic scheme laid out in the *Image*. Thus the first century, containing Joseph of Arimathea, corresponds with the white horse of the Apocalypse. Bale makes further links between the age of Simon Magus and the red horse, that of Pelagius and the black horse, and that of Dunstan and the pale horse (fols. 245ʳ⁻ᵛ). These correspondences are not very precise, and they may well have been imposed upon the material in retrospect. There is, however, a strongly patriotic flavor: "It is a wonder that Britain has always loved letters in spite of many great tribulations, and has flourished greatly in both languages" (fol. 2). At the beginning, Bale is careful to indicate the authorities he has used (fols. 1–2). He acknowledges that he has been able to consult libraries belonging to the Carmelites and Augustinians, but the Dominicans and others denied him (fol. 246ᵛ).

The individual lives follow the pattern noted above—a description of character in a brief biography, a bibliography with incipits, and some notes about historical context—but there are also many authorial comments which make Bale's views plain. He is especially appreciative of writers who did good work in times of depravity—writers like Bede, whom he compares to Lot among the Sodomites, and to the three boys in the fiery furnace (see Daniel 3:8–50; fol. 50). In the first century he is happy to include legendary material which he probably derived from Geoffrey of Monmouth, and this extends to the early legendary kings of Britain such as King Lucius (fol. 2ᵛ). That Bonducca Bellatrix (now usually known as Boadicea, Queen of the Iceni) is included is an indication of patriotism, even though her presence here does raise doubts about what Bale actually means by the term "writers." In this respect the work is an endorsement of a traditional view of history. Later, Bale's data are more directly taken from particular documents, and in this respect they become more factually reliable from a modern historical viewpoint.

Nevertheless, there is a rhetorical brilliance which appears in some of the portraits. Wyclif is placed at the beginning of the fourth century, which broadly addresses the period of great strife within the Church starting in the fourteenth century when the newer, and truer, faith fought with the older. Wyclif's description includes the following:

Illuxit enim ut stella matutina in medio nebulae ac diebus multis permansit testis in ecclesia fidelis. Quasi sol splendens in templo Dei refulsit et quasi thus ardens in igne. (fol. 154ᵛ)
[For he shone like the morning star in the middle of the darkness, and for many days he remained a faithful witness in the Church. He glittered like

the sun shining in the temple of God, and like incense burning in the
fire.]

The treatment of Wyclif may be used as an indication of how Bale
changed his material when he came to write the *Catalogus*. The scope of
his work is extended greatly in physical terms, but there is also a shift in
ideology as Bale turns more bitterly upon the papacy. Condemnation of
the latter was much less obvious in the *Summarium*. For example, in place
of "the baseness of the Antichrist" the *Catalogus* substitutes in the Wyclif
entry "the basenesses of the great whore." There are other changes in
wording which show how closely and carefully Bale revised the *Summarium* text in adapting it for the new role. Wyclif has been moved to be
the first in the sixth Century, as Bale had discovered many new items
from the late medieval period (good and bad) which he needed to incorporate.[15] The number of works he attributes to Wyclif increases from
154 to 238. He has found some new incipits as well as reassigning and
altering others. The last few lines of the *Summarium* entry are shifted in
the *Catalogus* to form part of the italicized appendices which are inter-
spersed throughout to make a continuous history of the papacy. This last
process also shifts the emphasis somewhat, since much of what is here
included is about the misdoings of the papacy on the Continent.

    The changes in the Wyclif entries described here can be paralleled in
countless ways in other entries in the *Catalogus*, even though in principle
the basis for the text is what Bale had already composed in the
Summarium. In the case of Bede, for example, the two versions are very
close, but the bibliography is increased from 96 to 142 items. The entry
on Alfred the Great is increased by two sentences which describe Alfred's
establishment of three colleges dedicated to grammar, philosophy, and
theology (*Summarium*, fol. 66; *Catalogus*, 126). On Bishop John Fisher,
Bale adds a sentence about his seditious resistance to King Henry VIII,
showing how he intended to extend the pernicious yoke of the purple
whore (*Catalogus*, 654). The additions to the Tyndale entry concern the
"mad and impious pseudo-bishop," Cuthbert Tunstall, who caused
Tyndale's translation of the most holy Testament to be burned in St.
Paul's churchyard in 1530. As Bale must have known about this when
he composed the *Summarium*, the addition is clearly polemical. Bale
makes many entirely new entries. Some, such as Caedmon, John Gower,
and Stephen Hawes are made to broaden the historical base. He also
pays close attention to recent victims of the Marian persecutions, adding
such martyrs as Nicholas Ridley and John Philpot, whose influence had

helped Bale's preferment in 1552. He adds details of the death of Cranmer and increases the number of Cranmer's works from three to 26 (three of these were written in prison).

The *Catalogus* remains a fascinating combination of noble aspiration (based, it must be emphasized, on much conscientious labor) with acrimonious and repetitive abuse. The latter may be justified by Bale in that he was writing from an embattled position (in exile) in which he feared his enemies would destroy him if they could. In the Introduction to the work there are passages where his eloquence does justice to the enormity of his task. He makes clear its great scope:

> *Descripsi autem non personarum tantum nomina sed et locorum ubi nati fuerunt: et Regum quorum patrociniis et auspiciis floruerunt: ut quid quisque scripserit et quae ingenii sui monumenta reliquerit et quo Servatoris nostri anno vixerit inde facili negotio intellegi percipique possit.* (sig. alpha 3)
>
> [I have described not so much the names of persons, but also the places where they were born and by the protection and guidance of which kings they flourished so that one could understand and perceive thence with little trouble what each wrote and what memorials of his wit he left, and in what year of our lord he lived.]

He identifies the need to rescue people from oblivion:

> *ubi annorum edax series consumet et omnis memoriae hostis delebit extinguetque oblivio.* (sig. alpha 3)
>
> [where the hunger of the years consumes lineage and where the enemy of all memory destroys and extinguishes with oblivion.]

He hopes to bring what has been saved before the attention of good and studious men:

> *vel a tineis ac vermibus corrosa vel malitia et invidia hominum de religione pessime iudicantium deformata atque dilacerata in tenebris caecaque caligine perierunt, in lucem vero atque noticiam hominum bonorum et studiosorum numquam aut raro prodierunt.* (sig. alpha 3)
>
> [even if they have perished by the gnawing of grubs and worms and by the malice and envy of judges of the worst religion, disfigured and torn apart in darkness and blind obscurity, they have appeared however into the light and into the knowledge of good and learned men never or rarely.]

The two bibliographical catalogs have been of great value to historians and scholars in other disciplines because they contain such a rich

accumulation of detail. They are especially valuable because Bale collected much of the information firsthand and because the collection is
unique. Although we have seen that this form of accumulation and presentation of information was not entirely his invention, it was Bale who
first addressed the British situation, and he did it in such a way that no
one has seriously rivalled him until, perhaps, the coming of the comput-
er age. His descriptions of personalities are also of interest, as, for example, in the generous way in which he praises the wit of the Catholic, John
Heywood.

At another level we may also note that Bale was part inheritor, part
creator of a cultural-historical tradition which no doubt fed Spenser,
Shakespeare and other Elizabethan poets, and by doing so, the main
British literary tradition. This is because Bale schematized history. He
did this in a number of ways through concepts like the "Image of Both
Churches" and through his sense of the continuity of English culture in
the face of foreign interventions. To a large extent his work became a history of British culture even though some of the details in it are now seen
to be patently wrong, and even though the particular ideology concerning the emergence of the Protestant church in England could not necessarily be shared either by all his contemporaries or by all who came after
him. In a way his historical work hovers between what we might now
call history and mythology, yet because he thought in the schematizing
and cyclic way that he did, others were no doubt led to formulate their
own patterns of history. Some of them, in addition to such a process,
have found the range and scope of Bale's information invaluable.

Even if some of the detail of his work has now to be dismissed
because it is inaccurate, or because his world view seems parochial,
there remains in his catalogs a complexity of comment and observation
which is deeply interesting, and this is especially true where he deals
with his contemporaries. In a way which he did not quite expect, he has
become an indispensable witness for his own times, and we are continu-
ally astonished in reading the catalogs by the sheer readibility of much
of his detailed writing.

Chapter Four
Three Laws

The discussion so far has indicated where the plays may have occurred in Bale's life and that they present some problems because text and performance do not necessarily appear to be the same. In the case of the plays printed in 1547 or 1548, the relationship to what Bale actually "compiled" in 1538 is obscure. The manuscript of *King Johan* shows beyond doubt that Bale reworked this text several times, often making meticulous alterations. In order to take full account of this, each chapter about the plays will begin with a brief account of the state of the text. This will be followed by sections on plot and character, and on language and verse. Each play will also be discussed in relation to its political and religious context. Consideration of the individual plays will be followed by chapters dealing with the staging of the plays, and with a general review of Bale's achievement.

Text

Three Laws, which was entitled in the first edition (?1548) *A Comedy concernynge Thre Lawes, of Nature, Moses, and Christ, corrupted by the Sodomytes, Pharysees and Papystes*, appears in all Bale's lists of his works, and it may well be the earliest extant. The subject matter in relation to the three Laws themselves seems very close to Tyndale's representation of them in his *The Obedience of a Christian Man* of 1528, a book which appealed greatly to Henry VIII as it conformed with his developing idea of royal supremacy. It may well be that the play was first written in the early 1530s as Bale adapted to Protestant beliefs. However, the evidence adduced for an original date of 1531 by Jesse W. Harris is not entirely convincing.[1]

There is of course no certainty that the play was actually performed in the 1530s, but the stage directions in the text show that Bale at least envisaged some aspects of production and may have seen fit to leave the items in the printed text. He certainly proposed a performance in Hampshire in 1551. However, all the stage directions are in Latin which perhaps makes it more likely that at the point of printing Bale had read-

A Comedy concer
nynge thre lawes, of nature
Moses, & Christ, corrupted
by the Sodomytes.
Pharysees and
Papystes,

Compyled by Johan Bale.
Anno M. D. XXXVIII.

FIG. 4   TITLE PAGE OF *Three Laws*

ers more in mind than performers. Some of them, such as those which designated the signs Deus Pater gives to each Law in Act I, and those about water, sword, and fire as a means of extirpating Infidelity in Act V, seem to have symbolic significance partly based upon scriptural meaning. At the other extreme some, but not all, exits are noted, including two which involve two people going out together, and there are directions about the songs. The costume instructions for Monachus, Necromatic, and Jurisconsultus are given at the first appearance of Sodomy, Idolatry, and Avarice, respectively (ll. 389, 399, and 907). If these seem to arise more conclusively from considerations of performance, their efficacy is nevertheless somewhat undermined because they are not used for all such occasions. When Infidelity gives instructions to Sodomy and Idolatry, there are five stage directions which show which of them he is addressing and may suggest physical movement or gesture (ll. 656–89). There is also a full instruction to begin the process of the clerical degrading of Lex Christi: "Here having removed his garment they put more shabby ones on him" (l. 1726 s.d., translated).

A further indication of performance is the doubling plan which appears at the end of the printed copy. Such a plan is rare during this period, and this is one of the first to survive; it may well mean that the play had been performed on tour with a company of five actors. The construction of the play is compatible with the scheme, and this degree of planning suggests that a performance was envisaged, as indeed do the description of the costumes that are to be worn by the vices:

> The aparellynge of the six vyces, or frutes of Infydelyte.
>
> Lete Idolatry be decked lyke an olde wytche, Sodomy lyke a monke of all sectes, Ambycyon lyke a byshop, Covetousnesse lyke a Pharyse or spyrit-uall lawer, False Doctryne lyke a popysh doctour, and Hypocresy lyke a graye fryre. The rest of the partes are easye ynough to conjecture.
>
> (Printed at the end of the play on sig. G1ᵛ)

These items may also imply that in publishing the play Bale hoped that others might perform it, an expectation in line with Protestant views of the efficacy of plays as a means of teaching. There is also a valuable indi-cation of the desirability of printing the plays. As the last section of the play begins Deus Pater gives Fides Christiani a role in the promulgation of his laws, and he adds, "Enprent their declaracyon / Of my swete promyses" (ll. 1932–33).

It is clear that Bale brought the play up to date during his exile in the Low Countries and Germany after 1540. The reference to Rugge and Corbet, who were, respectively, mayor and magistrate in Norwich in 1545, the time of Dorothy Bale's return to the city in the interests of her son, shows that Bale was concerned in revising so as to strike an immediately contemporary note. The reference to Wharton, the informer who served Cromwell and then served the more reactionary administration which followed, probably points in the same direction (ll. 1575–76). The last three stanzas of the text must have been written within ascertainable limits, for they refer to the "late" King Henry, who died in January 1547, and offer a prayer for Queen Catherine Parr, who lived until September 1548.

Plot

A consideration of the nature of the dramatic action of this and other extant plays by Bale may begin with the question of the relationship between theological intention and dramatic skill. The former gives some difficulty to the modern reader both for its intrinsic nature and for its place in the political history of the sixteenth century. But in spite of modern preferences which might regret the presence of such matters, there is no doubt that Bale meant to be polemical, to support what he thought was right and to destroy his enemies. And yet to try to separate out dramatic values on their own would probably be a barren and somewhat patronising exercise. The plays were written as acts of dramatic imagination, and that is something which cannot function in the abstract, not least because there is inevitably a hidden ideology to be taken account of, let alone the specific polemical purpose. The plays do not exist solely as polemical exercises: they invite a response in terms of language and of drama, and a full account of them cannot ignore the intimate connection between theatrical effectiveness and theological concepts.

The action of *Three Laws* is unique among Bale's extant plays in that the play follows the morality tradition solely. This is especially so since the plot is typical of the morality as it is invented to explain an intellectual concept of a theological nature. In Bale's other extant plays, including *King Johan*, following a different medieval tradition based upon an established story, the invention lies in the way the preexisting plot may be adapted and used by the dramatist. Here Bale is following a purely allegorical scheme which derives from both medieval and Reformation thinkers, but which operates primarily at a theoretical level. This leads to the significant patterning of the plot which is better appreciated as the working out of an intellectual concept rather than the telling of a story. The structure of the play is thus deeply committed to the didactic function, but this is one which also has a satisfying symmetry likely to appeal to a rational process.

The plot of the play depends upon the ubiquity of the Vice, here called Infidelity, who has operated from the time of Adam, and who has been specifically active in the periods of history which Bale chooses to reveal. The play has a five-act structure, though this is derived not so much from classical precedents as from the convenient structural principle in which he can use the first act to set up Deus Pater's purpose for the role of the three Laws of Nature, Moses, and Christ in history, the second through fourth acts each to show in turn the ways in which Infidelity damages each Law separately, and the fifth act to show the divine retribution (in the form of Vindicta Dei) upon Infidelity which restores the Laws to their former purity. This structure is repetitive, as each of acts 2, 3, and 4 shows a very similar process in which Infidelity uses two vices in each case, first to demonstrate their own character and extent, and then to damage each of the Laws. The only significant progress dramatically in these acts is that, following the interpretation of history adopted by Bale, there is development from Nature to Moses to the culmination in Christ. It is significant that the damage done to Christ, burning for heresy, is much more terrible than that done to the Law of Nature (leprosy) or the Law of Moses (blindness and lameness), thus reflecting the urgency with which Bale contemplated the religious strife of his own time. It is a powerful point that he actually uses burning to make clear the hostility of his enemies to the Gospel he sought to further.

The choice of particular incidents for each act is determined by Bale's historical construct for the play. It is related to what we have noted in the apocalyptic theology traceable in *Image*, but since *Three Laws* predates *Image*, it is not surprising that the form of history is not quite the same. It seems likely that Bale's particular blend of ideas is original, though it is clear that he has used ideas previously established by others. (The topic will be treated below more fully in the section on the religion and politics.) From the point of view of the plot, the vices can be aligned symmetrically with the three orders, and part of the function of the plot is to emphasize parallels as well as differences. Thus the three groups of vices can be described as the "fruits" of Infidelity, or as his children.

In general, *Three Laws* follows the common principle of the morality play in that its plot and action are designed to operate in a demonstrative way. A major part of the action is designed to give extensive opportunity for the characters, good and bad, to describe themselves and their activities. The audience's attitude to what is revealed has to be controlled so that the appropiate condemnation or approval will be elicited from them. In his role as their parent or master, Infidelity calls and introduces the vices. In the cases of Avarice and Ambition in act 3, Infidelity beats them into submission, but his promulgation of the influence of vices can also contain verbal comedy such as the exchange between the witch Idolatry and the homosexual Sodomy. Even if he approves them, he may employ a heartless mockery of them, a feature of his role which aligns him with the vice convention of later interludes and has the effect of stressing for the audience the implacable nature of evil. To be outraged by such behavior, however, is also to be entertained. The awfulness of villainy was and is compulsive viewing.

There is no doubt that sequences like these make up a very large part of the plot, but there are other important elements which enrich the didactic process. In the absence of the other vices, Infidelity has to attack the Laws, usually by mockery and a series of jokes which indicate that he is almost devilish in his approach. Indeed, there are a large number of references to the devil or devilish matters in the play, and frequently Infidelity is associated with them. At the beginning, Law of Nature calls him a "wycked fynde" (l. 361) and adds that he would shun the company of Infidelity as the devil of hell (ll. 372); in return Infidelity will make him "A morsell for the devyll" (l. 721). At the end when he is punished, Infidelity anticipates the traditional exit appropriate for devils and vices alike as he goes off to hell:

To the devyll of helle, by the messe, I wene I go. (l.1853)[2]

As we have no note of Infidelity's costume, there is no way of telling whether he looked like a devil. Perhaps his energetic performance in the role of a pedlar in act 3 suggests that he would not, as indeed does his apparent identification as a gray friar. He admits at l. 952 that he is not a "graye fryre" which suggests that he does look like one, as would his reported participation in the incident at the Franciscan friary in the Minories (ll. 807–8). The essence of his role is his adaptability; he uses his ability to adapt to others always with evil intention but also always in ways likely to draw attention himself. His role is theatrically the plum part, one demanding performing skills and the capacity to exploit the center of the stage in every possible way. We shall see that there are strong similarities between his part in the plot and that of Sedition in *King Johan*.

If the action contains many individual manifestations of Infidelity's versatility, there are other didactic procedures which must have had a significant stage presence. Though the damage done to the three Laws is carried out offstage, the reappearance of Law of Nature spotted with leprosy, and Law of Moses lame and blind, would be spectacular enough. The Law of Christ is managed differently in that a direction indicates that the despoiling of his garments, the initial step in the process of clerical degradation endured by many Protestant martyrs including Tyndale, is shown on stage (l. 1726 s.d.). He is then burned offstage, and he is restored visually by Deus Pater in the last act. His treatment is characterized as the most significant:

> In operacyon yet thu art the pryncypall. (l. 1897)

In reviving the Laws, Deus Pater refers to the signs given to each in act 1: the heart, the tables, and the New Testament (stage directions at ll. 112, 122, 134). The last act also contains the destruction of Infidelity by water, sword, and fire, these actions echoing scriptural items (Genesis 6:17, Leviticus 26:17, and Psalm 96:3). Since the didactic function is directed towards the restoring of the Laws and the punishment of Infidelity, the individual vices are not seen in the last act. No doubt their absence would partly be determined by the necessities of doubling, but it is also possible to see that the didactic purpose is faithfully pursued.

Character

The treatment of character is determined by principles similar to those underlying the plot. The characters are given scope to demonstrate their significance as a primary requirement. This may account for the specific note about costuming the vices quoted above. These costumes appear to be of an ecclesiastical origin, perhaps becoming available to players after the dissolution of monasteries which began in 1536, but the didactic point to be appreciated onstage was the association of such costumes with a corrupt group. Bale had a persistent inclination to interpret all papistical ceremonies and costumes as "juggling plays," evidently deceptions. However, since the action of this play is not so much the temptation of an everyman figure as a portrait of perennial corruption by vices, the characters, with the exception of God, are either victims or corrupters.

In presenting the evil characters, Bale exploits their theatricality in further ways. There is considerable variation of speech, especially in

Infidelity's long part. The other vices are differentiated by variations of verse forms and by the content of their discourse. For example, Avarice, an antagonist of the Law of Moses in Act III, who is dressed as "a Pharyse or spyrituall lawer," makes an attack upon the Decalogue, and will deceive by false ceremonies and a new creed. His objective is to obscure the true Law. This is sharply appropriate to the allegory since the underlying principle is that this particular age showed itself to be the one in which the strict and severe observance and enforcement of the law were required. In the process of such ridicule of what was correct, Bale is adept at bringing in accusations about the literal application of the law by papists, especially for venal purposes:

> For sylver and golde With falsehed I holde,
>   Supportynge every evyl.
> I have it in awe For to choke the lawe,
>   And brynge all to the devyll.
>   (ll. 1084–87)

In the speeches of Idolatry against the Law of Nature in act 3, Bale takes the opportunity for a lively attack upon superstitious remedies for all manner of illnesses, discomforts, and difficulties. These include help with baking and brewing (ll. 450–57), as well as with wells, ploughing, and the millstone. Indeed, Bale gives an interesting insight here into the way superstition was interwoven into everyday lives, a fact which is becoming more and more apparent. The patter of Idolatry is made all the richer because she has apparently changed sex and claims to give much help to women's problems, especially those related to motherhood and the health of children. She has many remedies for sicknesses, and also, it appears, for managing animals:

> With blessynges of saynt Germyne,
> I wyll me so determyne
> That neyther foxe nor vermyne
>   Shall do my chuckens harme.
> For your gese seke saynt Legearde,
> And for your duckes saynt Lenarde,
> For horse take Moyses yearde,
>   There is no better charme.
>   (ll. 507–14)

The relationship between Deus Pater and Vindicta Dei is not absolutely clear from the text; notably, the two are marked to be doubled.

However, there is virtually no time for a costume change at the critical moment in act 5 (from l. 1851 to l. 1854 on Infidelity's departure for hell), and it seems likely that Bale really intended these to be the same character, perhaps with different aspects, which could indeed be suggested by the simplest and most rapid of changes such as the changing of an overgarment or wings or a crown. If this were done in full view of the audience the symbolic link between the vengeful God and the beneficient Father would be established. Significantly Deus Pater begins, "As ye have seane here how I have strycken with fyre . . . (l. 1854). Such a link would be an interesting anticipation of the interrelationship between characters in *King Johan*, where abstract evils such as Sedition are made to manifest themselves as particular historical persons— Stephen Langton, Archbishop of Canterbury, in this case.

Language and Verse

A consideration of Bale's language in *Three Laws* will depend upon various inherited characteristics which he chose to follow, and also upon some innovative features. These latter give an indication of Bale's authorial intention and perhaps some implications about his concept of his audience, or audiences. Whatever detail one might adduce in these matters, it seems time to recognize that the overall effect of his language is one of vigor and versatility, including especially a reliance upon demotic speech for certain characters and for certain situations. The inherited factors have to do with Bale's education as a Carmelite, and embody a number of traditional rhetorical devices. There is also a polemical element, as Bale aligns himself with a number of significant Protestant, or perhaps Wycliffite, predecessors. Of these, there seems little doubt that Tyndale was the most important. Bale saw him as first in England after Wyclif.[3]

Because *Three Laws* is concerned with the clash between Infidelity on the one hand and Deus Pater and the Laws on the other, the speech contrasts between these parties are made very distinctive. Infidelity's role as a vice means that he must undermine the other characters as much as possible by mockery, and also by creating no doubt about the nature of his own evil ways: it is clear that language provides one of the most important identifying characteristics here and that it is used to direct the audience's attention to specific intentions.

Infidelity's part is most notable for its many demotic elements. Bale uses a number of regional characteristics which can be seen to derive from the East Anglian speech in which he had no doubt been reared.

This shows itself in such words as "shurne" (l. 371), "plawe" (l. 405), "blazings" (l. 431), "credle" (l. 471), "pylche" (l. 900—jerkin), and "sosse" (l. 1541). Most of these words can be traced to the *Promptorium Parvulorum*, a dictionary of East Anglian provenance dating from the fifteenth century, or to the Paston Letters. Closely connected with this use of East Anglian speech is Bale's use of the stage rustic speech for the witch Idolatry (ll. 400–2).

Bale makes much use of proverbial expressions. This topic is of great interest in early drama, which in general is rich in them. In Bale's case the deliberate exploitation of characters of low class and rustic background makes their use especially effective. However, it is important not to identify proverbs solely with this social group, for we can see in the case of John Heywood, whose audiences were largely at Court, that they had a stong appeal to the elite as well. Proverbs offer witty compression, encapsulated potted wisdom, and, perhaps most important, a means of access to the audience through known patterns of thought and speech. As an example, the following lines by Infidelity, challenging Law of Nature's contention that all things follow naturally strict laws, illustrate the tone of his expression and contain five proverbs or proverbial expressions:

> Now will I prove ye a lyar,
> Next cosyne to a fryar
>   And on the gall ye rubbe.
> Ye saye they folowe your lawe,
> And varyee not a strawe,
>   Whych is a tale of a tubbe. (ll. 274–79)

The abiding impression of such witty and cunning speech is that the speaker is up to no good. The possible "love" between Sodomy and Idolatry—something which has a place in the context of Bale's continuing attack upon the sexual mores of the religious orders—is expressed in grotesque language which draws upon proverbs and demotic speech:

Sodomy:	It is myne owne swete bullye,	[*lover*]
	My muskyne and my mullye,	[*endearments*]
	My gelover and my cullye,	[*gillyflower*]
	Yea, myne owne swetehart of golde.	
Infidelity:	I saye yet not to bolde.	
Idolatry:	Peace, fondelinge, tush a button.	

Infidelity: What wylt thu fall to mutton   [lechery]
               And playe the hungry glutton,
               Afore thys cumpanye?
               Ranke love is full of heate;
               Where hungry dogges lacke meate
               They wyll durty puddynges eate
               For want of befe and conye. (ll. 478–90)

There is implied action here, as Sodomy makes advances to Idolatry and is rejected.

In the passages as well, the colloquial tone of Infidelity's speech as he attempts to ridicule Law of Nature is further enhanced by mock obsequiousness: "I wolde so rubbe your botes . . ." (l. 210); a kiss-my-arse joke (l. 216), abusive name calling, "syr huddypeke" (l. 227); and an elaborate pun upon old cook and cock-old (ll. 235–43). This last word game goes on much too long and so is not very funny, which is presumably the point of its inclusion. Again we get a strong impression that such extremely vigorous language could be accompanied by all sorts of physical antics.

Since the doctrinal core of the play is the exposition of God's laws, Bale turns to authorities which support or generate his views.[4] As references to classical writers are comparatively rare in Bale's plays, the inclusion of Cicero and Chrysippus by the Prolocutor is remarkable both as a reaching for authority in support and for its stylistic strength in a keynote speech; but the chief authority and example for Bale was Tyndale, who after 1530 placed more and more emphasis upon the Law of God, as we have noted. Bale's intellectual and theological debts to Tyndale will be treated more fully in the next section. Here it is relevant to note that Bale follows Tyndale's language in a number of places in *Three Laws*. Bale seems to have followed him in using similar imagery over the wells of Abraham, the removal of the veil from the face of Moses, and the use of the four knights as a means of burying Christ or the Gospel. There is also close similarity in vocabulary—for example, in the use of "apysh" (l. 1328) and "domme" (l. 1246). Such echoes may well be seen as a political language whereby reformers sought to align themselves and to proclaim the authority of their readings, especially of scripture.

Bale's quotation from Mantuanus (ll. 1848–49) may be seen in a similarly polemical light, for Mantuanus, although a Carmelite, offered Bale a criticism of the order from within which he obviously valued and developed in several of his works. There are also links with the Bible itself as in "paynted tumbes" (l. 1710) which give similar force to Bale's language. He has a good ear for such expressions, and while one may not necessarily agree or sympathize with the tone of his language, it may be appreciated as an effective form of dramatic speech, especially in the context of persecution and uncertainty in which he was working. Even the abuse of his enemies can be skillfully done and can offer scope for actors in terms of language as well as action:

> Thys congregacyon   is the true church mylytaunt;
> Those counterfet desardes   are the very church malygnaunt.
>   (ll. 1355–56)

It seems that we ought to be skeptical of views which dismiss Bale's achievement: even Thora Blatt, who has written the most comprehensive study of his style, falls into the temptation of describing his plays as moving by means of "talk only" when in fact much of this extremely vigorous language has a strength in itself and seems also likely to prompt lively activity onstage. We need to revalue such throwaway comments as: "we shall consider the art—or lack of it—with which sentences and words have been strung together."[5] It is through the vigor of the language, with its variety of allusion and its many changes of pace and register, that the formal structure of the play can be perceived as facilitating rather than inhibitive.

Turning to other stylistic elements in the play, there are many rhetorical devices which enhance the force of what is said. Patterns play a great part through such characteristics as repetition, balance (often with half-line contrast), syntactical inversion of sentences and phrases, and grouping of ideas in twos and (very commonly) threes. There is a good deal of alliteration at times, which brings these juxtapositions into greater effect. The following lines spoken by Vindicta Dei, deriving from Exodus 7:17–11:8, bring out these characteristics:

> Into Eqipte I brought   ten terryble ponnyshmentes
> Upon the people,   for breakynge hys commaundements.
> Their wholsom waters   I tourned into bloude;
> I multyplyed frogges   to poyson therwith their foude;
> I made waspes and dranes   them grevously to stynge,
> And all kyndes of flyes   sone after ded I in brynge;
> Upon their cattel   I threwe the foule pestylence,
> Bothe botche, byle and blayne   they had for their offence;

> Lyghtenynges and haylynges   destroyed their corne and frute;
> A swarme of hungry locustes their pastours destytute.
>
> (ll. 1793–1802)

This passage also relates to versification since the arrangement of rhetorical elements within the verse form, and within individual lines, is clearly part of the effect achieved. The formal structure is clarified by Bale's habit of marking the caesurae in his longer lines of verse. We shall have more to say on this in the versification of *King Johan*, but here it may be useful to note that Bale marked the caesurae in the printed texts of *Three Laws* by a comma.[6] The process has the effect of enhancing the balanced elements in the verse, and again one can see that the rhyme also contributes. The key places at the beginnings of lines and half-lines are exploited for rhythmic purposes, and to point up parallels—as with the use of the pronoun "I" in ll. 1795–99, above.

This play is notable for its variety of verse forms, and even if it were the earliest of Bale's extant plays, it suggests that he was already a very competent versifier. For the majority of serious speeches, and for some of the places where the vices attack the Laws in conversation, the standard verse is pentameter couplets. These can be split between speakers (a useful aid for prompts or cues?), but individual lines are not usually split internally, except by the caesurae as noted above. Often the second half of the line is an extension or modification of the sense of the first, but it may have a contrasting rising or falling cadence. This form is flexible and is successful in some strong dramatic moments.

There is even greater variety in the use of rhyme couée, a form which gives great speed and immediacy to the speeches of the vices. The stanzas quoted above, spoken by Infidelity, Idolatry, and Sodomy illustrate this. But the basic form (trimeters rhyming aabccb) can be made shorter or longer according to need, as is shown by the variation aaabcccbb above. The form can possibly have very short dimeters:

> I Covetyse am,   The devyll or hys dam,
>   For I am insacyate.
> I ravysh and plucke,   I drawe and I sucke,
>   After a wolvysh rate. (ll. 1060–36; original layout)

With such brevity and a regular structure it can be appropriate for Bale's frequent construction of lists, as in Sodomy's list of unnatural lovers, or Avarice's list of his followers (ll. 611–18, and ll. 1072–79).

Rime couée is plentiful in *Three Laws*, but it does not appear in the other extant plays.

The third verse form used by Bale here is the rhyme royal (pentameters rhyming ababbcc). Each line usually contains a caesura following the first two accented syllables, of which this line by Deus Pater is typical:

> A mercy, a goodnesse, a truth, a lyfe, a sapyence. (l. 3)

This is recognizable as a more exclusively formal and elevated type, and it is used sparingly. It is appropriate to the first few minutes of the play in which Deus Pater sets out formal relationships with the Laws, and it is used significantly to mark the change from the speeches of Vindicta Dei (as above) to Deus Pater in the last act. This form of verse is also used by Bale as Prolocutor in this and other plays. It is separate enough in itself to establish the special tone required for authoritative doctrinal speeches, and it has a particular strength in the last two lines which may form a summative couplet. An example of this occurs when Deus Pater is finally confirming the roles and symbols of each Law in act 5 at ll. 1884–1901. He addresses one stanza to each, beginning with the title ("Thu Lawe of Nature"), and each stanza ends with a couplet referring specifically to the appropriate sign. Thus for Moses we have:

> Lose not those tables whych are a token true,
> That thu in the flesh shalt evermore contynue (ll. 1894–95).

Religion and Politics

As the time when Bale was writing was one of intense public controversy it is difficult to separate religion from politics. The position is made more complex because Bale's religious purpose was to change by persuasion; he saw himself as an evangelist. Yet at the same time politics is about acquiring power in order to influence change. In these respects Bale's purposes overlap. We should also remember that the publication of a text may relate to political circumstances quite different from those in which it was initially performed, or indeed originally composed.

Bale's thinking about the nature of the three Laws can be shown to have both traditional Catholic precedents and specific Protestant elements centering upon the work of Tyndale. The concept of the three ages of the world may be found in the Venerable Bede (c. A.D. 672–735), an author whom, as already noted, Bale found congenial and whose works he at one time possessed. In any case, access to Bede would not have been difficult in a monastic library. In explaining the three masses for Christmas day, Bede divides the time of this world into three parts, "The first time before the law, the second under the law, and the third the time of grace." For the three Masses he explains that "the first is sung in the dark night for those . . . without the knowledge of God; the second in twilight for those who had knowledge of God through the law which was given and through the prophets, but it was not complete; the third is sung in full daylight for those in the new time to whom the full knowledge of God is made."[7] The same general concept may be found in other writers. A more developed example is in the twelfth-century text of John Belethus, *Rationale Divinorum Officiorum*, where the three ages are divided so that the first, before the Law, includes Adam, Noah, and Abraham; the second, under the Law, includes Moses, David, and the Exile of the Jews; and the third, the time of grace, includes the time of the apostles and evangelists, the time of persecution, and the time of peace.[8] The fifteenth-century *Speculum Sacerdotale* approximates more closely to Bale's formulation of the Laws. His terminology is foreshadowed:

> we dyvyde alle the tyme of this world by thre tymes. The firste tyme is that [that] was of natural lawe fro Adam unto Moyses. The secounde tyme is of writen lawe that was fro Moyses unto the advent of oure lord. The thridde tyme is tyme of grace that is fro the advent unto the ende of the world.[9]

Upon this traditional basis Bale elaborated ideas from the Bible and probably from Tyndale's interpretation of it. The importance of his wish to schematize history cannot be doubted, and it leads to the more apocalyptic interpretation he later developed in *Image*: this is forshadowed at ll. 1861–70. There is, however, no one passage in Tyndale's work which has emerged as a specific source, suggesting that Bale's method was one of "compilation," arranging material to suit his particular thesis. It is notable too that although the play is written to such an objective in the convention of a morality, his treatment of history allows him access to the legendary or historical material of biblical narrative by way of illustration.

Bale specifically combined the notion of the three ages with the three Laws, and he also was influenced by Tyndale's understanding of human beings. Although Bale avoids the common morality-play practice of having a central human character who is attacked by evils and defended by virtues, he wanted to show that the Christian may be inwardly corrupted:

"And hys nature is full bryttle and unsure" (l. 756). In this he may have been influenced by Tyndale:

> Now are there thre natives of men, one all together beestly which in no wise receave the lawe in their heartes . . . them that worsheped the golden calfe . . . The seconde are not so beestlye and unto the lawe cometh: but they loke not Moyses in the face . . . Kepe they the lawe outwardly with workes but not in the herte . . . The thred are spirituall and loke Moyses in the open face and are (as Paul saith the seconde to the Romans) a lawe unto them selves and have the lawe written in their hertes by the spirite of God.[10]

The essence of Bale's treatment of the Laws, underlined by such imagery as that in this passage, is that the Law of Moses was the most severe, giving punishment after the time of exile: it was followed by reconciliation under the Law of Christ. The presentation of the sign of the heart to Law of Nature stresses Bale's concern for the inner Christian, but this is balanced by the external images which operate in the main actions of the play, especially in the fate which overcomes the Laws at the end of each act. Sodomy, attacking the Law of Nature, says:

> I wyll corrupt God's Image
> With most unlawfull usage. (ll. 683–84)

For these images, Bale was probably again relying upon scriptural sources and Tyndale's interpretation. The affliction of leprosy upon Law of Nature is in line with the biblical punishment for sin in the Old Testament. Blatt adduces Numbers 12:9–11 and Leviticus 13 (137). Blindness may be derived from Deuteronomy 28:28–29. As T. W. Craik notes, the restoring of Moses is a Protestant application of II Corinthians 3. Significantly, Tyndale's comment leads into Bale's political background as Christ "plucketh away from the face of Moses, the vaile which the Scribes and Phareises had spred thereon."[11]

It also seems likely that Craik is right in suggesting that the full title of Tyndale's work on Matthew gives a significant hint to a political purpose of Bale: *An exposition upon the V.VI.VII chapters of Mathew, which three chapters are the keye and the dore of the scripture, and the restoring agayne of Moses law corrupte by the Scribes and Pharises. And the exposition is the restoring agayne of Christes lawe corrupte by the Papistes.*

The political intention is an attack upon Catholic prelates who obscure the true law as Bale saw it, in parallel to the Scribes and

Pharisees. There can be little doubt that this was a strong concern for Bale during his first exile when he sharpened his attack upon the conservative Henrician bishops. The abuses by the the Vices in acts 2 and 3 are spread over a longer period of history, but in Act IV the attacks become more contemporary in accordance with the emphasis upon the time of Christ. The difficulty of determining a precise date for *Three Laws* has already been indicated. This makes a close political placing of the play more difficult. The strongest indications are, however, the doctrines and imagery of Tyndale, who was publishing in the late 1520s and early 1530s. This accords with what we can be reasonably sure of, that the play is the earliest extant by Bale. However, the references to Rugge, Corbet, and Wharton (ll. 1575–76) suggest that when Bale was reworking the play in the 1540s he saw some point in localized East Anglian allusion at the time when he was in exile and may have wanted to influence the conservative climate of King Henry's later years. In general terms it seems likely that in the absence of a more specific context the play is not so committed to political circumstances as some of the lost plays, such as the one about the king's two marriages, and as we shall find to be the case with *King Johan*.

Bale was perhaps more concerned in *Three Laws* with establishing a general theoretical base. To this end he focuses through the Vices upon what he might have called longer-term abuses by the Catholic church, as well as the appropriately positive program for Protestantism. For the former he mounts a spectacular attack upon celibacy, the monastic orders, the distortion of the scriptural truths he perceived, and pardons (in which Infidelity links the trade of pardoner with that of pedlar). For the latter the introduction of Fides Christiana near the end of the play is a symbolic act which summarizes the doctrine. With his encouragement the three Laws set out their respective effects of knowledge, worship, and love (ll. 1965–85), and he expresses hope:

> Now the lyght is come the darknesse dyeth awaye;
> I trust in the Lorde men wyll walke in the daye. (ll. 1991–92)

The fate of Law of Christ (Evangelium) on stage is that he is to be burned (l. 1731), no doubt as an example of the martyrdom of some of Bale's contemporaries. However, some earlier lines seem to suggest that he may be buried; that his grave may be stamped on; and that four knights, representing prelates, covetous lawyers, ignorant lords, and unjust judges, may be appointed to guard the tomb in a way similar to the incident in the Resurrection episodes of the Corpus Christi plays (ll. 1565–66). There may be an inconsistency here, arising perhaps from the revision of the text (the passage is quite close to that referring to Rugge, Corbet, and Wharton), but the symbolic importance of both deaths is relevant to Bale's objectives. On the one hand, the Law of Christ is subject to burning, and on the other, the persecution is an echo of the persecution and death of Christ at the hands of the Scribes and Pharisees. In the words of False Doctrine,

> As he preached here, we followed from place to place
> To trappe him in snare, and hys doctryne to deface. (ll. 1555–56)

Thus it appears that *Three Laws*, as we have it in its printed form, is not sharply focused on particular historical events: Bale's targets are the more general abuses of the Catholic Church, with a special animus against the clergy. There is a striking originality, or at least a remarkably comprehensive power of synthesis, in the way Bale combines various manifestations of blasphemy, heresy, and idolatry from the Fall of Adam to the 1540s. The play is the work of one who realized an ideology in the perceived structure of history, and the subsequent use of historical material in *King Johan* and in *Image* flows naturally from it. The play's dramatic qualities are closely in tune with the symbolic, emblematic, and satirical strength of allegory that can be found in the earlier morality plays, but there is an overriding urgency to show the triumph of Christian Faith over Infidelity, the Vice of the play.

Chapter Five
King Johan

Text

In spite of the qualities of *Three Laws*, Bale's *King Johan* is probably his most successful surviving play, and the one which has attracted most attention. It contributes much to our understanding of sixteenth-century drama because of the striking originality of its invention; because of its practicality as a stage play; and because of the insights it allows into the relationship between religion, politics, and the stage. Before a consideration of these, however, an account must be given of the nature of the remarkable manuscript by which the play has come down to us. The manuscript is a highly complex but intrinsically fascinating matter which will be summarized here. Its importance lies in what it reveals about Bale's procedures as a playwright, and in the way the play fits into the evolving Reformation.

In modern times, the manuscript emerged in 1838 and was published then by J. P. Collier. Collier claimed that it was found at Ipswich, though this has not been substantiated.[1] Primarily, it is the work of an experienced scribe (scribe 'A'), who was transcribing from a copy, presumably by Bale himself. When he had finished, he revised the copy—which is usually known as the A text—in a number of ways which will become apparent. Later Bale himself undertook a wholesale revision of the manuscript, making many interventions on the sheets written by scribe A. However, about three-quarters of the way through, Bale decided he would recopy the end of the play completely, no doubt because his changes were becoming more and more extensive. He rejected the last sheets of scribe A's version and substituted his own, on quarto pages instead of folio. He also interpolated two quarto leaves into the earlier part of the A text. The parts of the A text he allowed to stand, together with the revisions, make up a coherent and apparently complete play. In all probability Bale was transcribing from sections newly drafted, and this revision constitutes the B text. Fortunately two rejected leaves (four sides of writing) from near the end of the A text, partially crossed through by Bale, have been recovered. They overlap with Bale's revised text for 359 lines (ll. 1803–2161), but they do not extend to the original ending of the A text, which now can only be conjectured. It is clear from these rejected sheets that Bale incorporated virtually every line of the A text into the B version.

Because there is no change in the style of the work from the A text to the B, there is no reason to doubt that the whole of what survives represents Bale's work, and his alone, written at two or more different times, except, of course, for minor revisions by scribe A. There is some difficulty in deciding the date of composition—exactly when the A text was copied and when Bale set about his revisions. Some external evidence enables us to narrow conjecture, however, even though an exact answer as to when the two versions were written escapes us. *King Johan* appears in all four of Bale's lists of his plays. The earliest, in *Anglorum Heliades*, is dated 1536 on the same page, even though it is apparent that other parts of this document were revised up until at least 1539, and we cannot therefore be quite sure that the earlier date was the correct one. In the A text itself there is a reference (which is not an interpolation) to the burning of the painting on wood of the image from Wales of Darvell Gathyron at Smithfield in May 1538 (l. 1229), which means that this copy at least, if not the original play, must postdate that event. Because the entry in *Anglorum Heliades* refers to "two books" of *King Johan*, and because there is no sign in the A text of a division, it does seem likely that there was an earlier divided, and perhaps longer, version. Some of the revisons by A, mentioned above, are changes or additions to the stage directions, including some quite elaborate but partially unworkable arrangements for doubling, which suggests that his version was related to a performance, though it could be in anticipation or in retrospect. As it happens, there are indications of a performance in September 1538 at St. Stephen's in Canterbury, and there may have been another performance of a play about King Johan at Christmastide 1538 in Cranmer's house. Cromwell made a payment at the end of January 1539 to "Balle and his ffelowes for playing before my lorde" which may refer to the latter performance, though the entry does not mention the play by name.[2] It will be seen from the consideration of the political context of the play below, however, that this period, from the end of 1538 into early 1539, is perhaps the most likely time for the preparation of the A text.

With regard to the B text, the date of the revision again eludes us. At the very end, beyond the overlap noted above, there are six stanzas which contain a reference to Queen Elizabeth's policy on the Anabaptists. These stanzas must date from after 22 September 1560, by

which time Bale had returned from exile to Canterbury. This date contrasts with an earlier passage which manifestly predates this action.[3]
Thus the main revision may have been done before 1560, and Bale may
have done some last-minute tidying up, either for a performance or for
publication. A reference to "our late kynge Henrye" makes it likely that
Bale did not begin the revision until after Henry's death in 1547.[4] This
is corroborated by Bale's handwriting in the manuscript. As mentioned
in chapter three, he adopted the habit of putting a tick over the letter
u/v after he went into his first exile in 1540,[5] and since this trait appears
in the B revision, it is likely that the revision, if not the exemplum from
which it came, followed his departure. Since the paper he used for the
long, revised sequence leading up to the ending is all of the same type, it
also seems likely that the copy, if not the composition of the revisions,
was made in one continuous effort after 1558, incorporating the
Elizabethan addition.

Thus the two versions of the play may very well have been written at
widely separated times in Bale's life. The A text and its possible prede-
cessor most probably come from the 1530s when Bale was more dis-
cernibly engaged in the performance of plays. The B text may relate
more clearly to some point after the end of the first exile. These broad
conclusions may be further supported by a brief consideration of the
kinds of changes made in the revisions.

As noted above, scribe A's revisions are very much concerned with
stage directions. As he copied the play he left spaces in the form of boxes
in midline for the insertion of stage directions. A study of the inks used
makes it clear that he subsequently filled, or even overfilled, some of
these boxes. He left some others blank, however, as though he never
could decide or find out what should be written there. His other corrections are mainly to incidentals of spelling or other copying errors, but it
is interesting that he was unsystematic about this, and he usually made
corrections on pages to which his attention was drawn by the necessity
to attend to the stage directions.

Bale's alterations and additions to the A text were more far-reaching.
He was more systematic than scribe A, and was obviously intervening
for all sorts of different reasons which cannot be summarized in a simple
way, though it is clear that in most respects he was furthering polemical
objectives. In terms of performance he seems to have accepted scribe A's
stage directions and the modifications to them, but he shows indifference
to improving or completing them. For new material he does add some
perfunctory directions, but he does nothing specific about doubling

except make his additions compatible. If he does not seem very concerned about performance itself, he is nevertheless keenly interested in what might be called dramatic effect. To this end he elaborates the part of Sedition as the Vice, perhaps in the light of appearances of more and more examples of this conventional type between the two versions. Thus Sedition acquires a noisy offstage outburst, a passage of laughter, and a more definitely conspiratorial role.[6]

Bale also divides the play into two acts, and adds the Interpretour who makes a number of typological links between Bale's contemporaries and scriptural figures. He strengthens the role of Johan, adding explanation and justification for some of his acts; traditionally Johan had an unenviable reputation, and Bale was under some necessity to improve it. He sharpens up the satires upon relics and upon the monastic orders by adding a goodly number of items to existing lists.

Less concerned with polemical matters is perhaps Bale's persistent, but incomplete, attempt to remove some features of East Anglian spelling from the A text—for example, 25 changes of the ending "-onde" to "-ande" (as in "Ynglonde" to "Englande"). As scribe A was apparently copying, it is possible that these dialect elements were Bale's own originally, though scribes inevitably used their own dialect at times. Bale is even more meticulous in his alterations to the pointing of the verse. In nearly every line of scribe A's manuscript, he changes the raised point marking the caesura to a comma, and he sometimes corrects the rhythm by moving the comma to a different place in the line. As this midline comma is found in the printed texts of the other plays, it seems likely that this aspect of the revisions was directed toward printing, but the accumulation of the revisions does not point exclusively to either print or performance.

Plot

Bale's managing of both plot and character is innovative. This is not to say that in either case he does not use some of the traditions of the morality drama, but it is clear that he was not content simply to follow them. Even though his main work on the history of England was yet to come, he already saw that historical events could be regarded as cyclic and that patterns were discernible. Such a view of history might possibly have been perceived in the mystery cycles, in which figurative elements that anticipate or recall parallels, as between Adam and Christ, or the Flood and the Last Judgment, are a structural feature, but Bale departed from this in choosing a secular subject, a selected part of the life of King Johan.

From the morality plays Bale may have inherited an essentially comedic structure: a design which led to a rounded conclusion in which evil was punished and good rewarded, the plot passing through vicissitudes which, by their figurative nature, imposed a moral pattern upon human experience. The allegory, bringing into the plot a fixed structure, gave various forms to this process, usually by reference to some formalized pattern such as a pilgrimage or the coming of death. In *King Johan* this is played out in that the moral evils led by Sedition are eventually punished by the powers of virtue, and Johan himself is vindicated. The departures from this approach, however, are momentous in that Johan dies not as a result of a moral fault, but as the victim of various destructive and evil forces. The death of heroic figures had occurred before in the moralities, as with Humanum Genus in *The Castle of Perseverance*, but they were usually guilty and needed divine mercy to restore them to grace.

The attraction of Johan as a hero was chiefly his oppositon to the papacy which brought excommunication upon him. The idea was perhaps prompted by Tyndale's *Obedience*, in which the chief characteristic in Johan's fate is that he encounters the conspiracies of the papacy manifested in releasing the nobles from their allegiance to the crown, in attending to the legal privileges of the clergy, and in preparing a military onslaught upon England. Tyndale also points up a leading theme in Bale's play: "Was not kinge John fayne to delyver his crowne unto the legate and to yeld up his realme unto the Pope wherfore we pay Peter pence?" (fols. 157[r-v]) As we shall see, this theme of the supremacy of the King against the papacy was fundamental to the political struggles of the late 1530s.

The purpose of the play, largely political as it is, also has its religious side in that Bale saw in Johan the opportunity of creating an example and a martyr for the Protestant cause. It is significant that in the revisions Bale found it necessary to incorporate new material which strengthened Johan's virtuous and heroic response to the conspiracies against him, and also to make the death scene more pathetic. The king's responses to what happens to him also take the form of doctrinal exposition akin to preaching, which suggests that for Bale the ideal of kingship included the need to spread the Gospel. The creation of this example is made more complex as the real King John had a bad reputation which Bale had to negotiate in order to present his ideal king. In this process of amendement he was supported by other Protestant sources.[7]

Bale constructs an allegory of deception and death by making Johan defend the plight of the widow England, separated from God, her husband, by the perversions of Catholicism. This position sets off a series of exposures of the wickedness of the clergy even before the plot really gets under way. It is managed largely by the intervention of Sedition, who ridicules and abuses England, though she is able to give as good as she gets in abuse, calling the clergy the Pope's pigs (l. 119).

Bale's later division of the A text into two acts indicates that the purpose of the first is to set up the conspiracy against Johan, while the second shows its working out, followed by divine restoration. The plot is managed by constant movement between the historical narrative with its accompanying historical data (though these data are of course limited by Bale's ideological intentions, as well as by the nature of the sources), and the allegorical structure, which points always to the death of a martyr. The allegory is enhanced by the roles of the three estates characters, Nobility, Clergy, and Civil Order, upon whom Johan relies for good government. Such temptation as there is in the play is directed against these characters by Sedition, who tries to undermine their support for the King, and it is they who fluctuate morally in response to his attacks. The first act shows them uneasy but submitting to Johan. While Nobility, an engaging class portrait of a rather thick but loyal warrior, seems to embody patriotic support, and Civil Order behaves correctly, Clergy is the most volatile, quick to find fault behind the King's back but also kneeling in submission. Nobility and Clergy debate the issue of loyalty in terms of the scriptural motif of what is owed to Caesar.

The management of the group of evil characters turns largely upon an elaborate process of setting up relationships, which are of course allegorical. Sedition shows that he is the cousin of Dissimulation who, by his costume, a mixture of items from different monastic orders, is another manifestation of the clergy, but one who differs in function from the character so named. Without a direct indication of the change of location, these two are suddenly found to be in Rome where they take part in an elaborate allegorical theatrical set piece. Dissimulation brings in Private Wealth; Private Wealth brings in Usurped Power, who in turn brings in Sedition. Though there is some sense of being at Rome, the action or "gere" (Sedition's word at l. 770) by which this is demonstrated is presented on an abstract plane, as the action shows Sedition carried in by the other three: "Here they shall bare hym in" (stage direction at l. 802). This is played with ludicrous and scatological decoration but probably is meant to parody the carrying in of a bishop to his enthronement. However, in theatrical terms the sequence is more resonant because it quickly becomes apparent that Sedition really is a bishop; he is Stephen Langton seeking to become Archbishop of Canterbury. By the same token, Usurped Power admits he is the Pope, even though he is at the moment in "lyght apparell" (l. 868, and compare l. 834).

The sense of the relationships between these evil characters, whether historical or allegorical, is cemented by extensive musical elements, backed up by liturgical parody.[8] On entry, Usurped Power and Private Wealth sing part of Psalm 136 ("Super flumina Babilonis" at ll. 764–65, with a word changed by Bale to suggest they pursue their own good rather than God's). When the carrying in is complete, they all sing another, unspecified song (l. 828). This occurs before the audience is told who they are. It is here that Dissimulation, who is a bit slow, suddenly realizes that he is in the presence of the Pope. Possibly, because of the music, the audience would have got there first, or at least had an inkling, but it is an effective theatrical discovery.

The point of the visit to Rome can now be enacted: Dissimulation is a messenger from the English clergy, come to bring complaints against Johan to the Pope. The response of the latter is to take the first steps toward excommunication, and in order to do this he goes off to dress in the papal regalia, while Private Wealth dresses as the Cardinal. These manifestations are not meant to operate as disguises, but to carry an allegorical link by which the Pope is seen as an embodiment of Usurped Power, and the Cardinal (later called Pandulphus) as Private Wealth.

The structure of the second act is more complicated, perhaps because of the expansion, but Bale's device of shifting between historical and allegorical resonances for his characters undoubtedly enriches the dramatic texture. This would perhaps be less difficult to interpret in performance where the physical appearance and gestures of the actors would make some aspects more specific. Bale was highly selective in his use of information about King Johan. The aspects which interested him are the working out first of the interdiction upon the English people, followed by the papal demand for Johan's submission, his resignation of the crown, and his death. The action of the play, however, shows how this is revealed by means of the abstract characters who are sometimes in historical mode and sometimes not. There is no attempt to relate all the scenes in which they are involved to historical counterparts.

Thus the second act begins with Nobility's confession, in the Catholic rite, to Sedition. Although the latter says he comes from the Pope, he does not call himself Steven Langton here; indeed, he assumes briefly the alias Good Perfection, directly in the tradition exemplified by Skelton's vices in *Magnyfycence*.[9] It is only on completion of this confession that Sedition admits to being Langton in order to receive the submission of Clergy and Civil Order (they kneel to him at l. 1192). There follows the ostensibly historical sequence in which there is no doubt that Private Wealth is dressed as a Cardinal (l. 1303 s.d.) come to threaten Johan, and subsequently to curse him with bell, book, and candle when he refuses to submit. Bale, however, emphasizes that the refusal turns on Johan's unwillingness to accept Langton, and it is clear that we are meant to think of the latter as Sedition as well.

After the curse, Clergy, Nobility, and Civil Order are united in their hostility to Johan: Nobility, upon whom much depends, is pointedly afraid to be seen with him (ll. 1447–48). The state of the country is exemplified by the appearance of Commonalty, who is blind because he lacks knowledge of the Gospel. The pressure mounts upon Johan, who out of compassion for his people decides to submit. He surrenders the crown and gives a written obligation to carry out the Pope's commands (stage directions at ll. 1728 and 1778). Thus the issue of royal supremacy is dramatized in the play by showing Johan forced to relinquish his authority.

For the next two incidents Bale had some support from the chronicles, but in each case he adds an allegorical reference. The clerk who was apprehended for clipping the coinage appears as Treason, and is saved by the Church. The death of Johan himself, as described by some accounts which Bale chose to follow, is caused by poison administered by the monk, Simon of Swineshead. In this incident we meet the poisoner first as the already familiar Dissimulation, who then makes it clear that he is Simon. His aspirations to sainthood, since he must drink half the draught before Johan, are comically presented by associating him with Becket.

With the end of the historical material, Bale turns to an allegorical resolution, but this is interestingly given a contemporary gloss. Veritas tells Bale's truth about Johan, especially his role as a king serving God. This revelation is followed by admissions of error by Clergy, Civil Order, and Nobility, who appear to be unchanged from their earlier function and are still not identifiable as "real" people. The final movement of the play is dominated by Imperial Majesty, who must be a kingly figure, and who exiles Private Wealth and Usurped Power. The treatment of Sedition is more extensive. He is no longer Langton, but he tries yet another alias, Holy Perfection—to no avail. He is sentenced to be hanged and quartered, and his head is to be placed upon London Bridge (ll. 2579–84). This conclusion to the plot draws heavily upon morality conventions, and it perhaps contributes substantially to them. The behavior of Sedition is evil to the end, but he is also ridiculous, as evil characters so often are in the moralities.

Character

It will be evident from this account of the plot that Bale's innovation with regard to character is intimately related to his decision to choose a secular and historical narrative and to use it in a partly allegorical manner. We are able to see the evil characters as primarily abstract forces who are loose in a kind of moral stratosphere and who become manifest as specific historical characters, or rather as historical characters in the version of history which expresses Bale's polemical purpose. The implication is that Sedition, Usurped Power, Private Wealth, and, to a lesser extent, Treason, are perennial evils. Bale's real purpose is to place grim but also grotesque emphasis upon their powerful threat to Church and state in his own time. The critical point to note here is that, by Bale's method, the characters acquire an extra dimension which can be called upon as required. This extra dimension, expressed in the visual terms of the performed drama, is perhaps one of the reasons why the drama offers special advantages to the polemicist. It gives importance to the self-explanation which is an inherent part of the morality mode, but it also allows dangerous or delicate real-life significances to be obliquely suggested.

The allegorical mode also encourages a strong sense of the particular, a kind of realism which makes some aspects of a highly abstract mode engagingly real. We have noted the bluff honesty of Nobility, and this can be illustrated further in the scene in which he and the other two estates submit to Veritas. The differences between his straightforwardness, the complaisance of Clergy, and the caution of Civil Order are quite plain:

Veritas:	But are ye sorye for thys ungodly wurke?
Nobylyte:	I praye to God, els I be dampned lyke a Turke.
Veritas:	And make true promyse ye wyll never more do so?
Clergye:	Sir, never more shall I from true obedyence goo.
Veritas:	What saye yow, brother? I must have also your sentence.
Cyvyle Order:	I wyll ever gyve to my prynce due reverence. (ll. 2309–14)

Although these characters are social types rather than abstractions, they are not meant to be specific individual persons of the time. As such they have resonance in Bale's contemporary scene, and it looks as though one of the purposes of the play was to influence different groups within the nation. The action of the play reveals all three as vulnerable, and we have noted that it is they who are really the target for seduction by the vices led by Sedition. Under his attack, all give way in regard to their duties and their loyalty to the King. As we shall see, it is likely that there is a particular political context for this, at one point at least, in the play's evolution.

The character of King Johan is different from the others. He is meant to be a specific historical character, though we have noted that a good deal of what might have been attributed to him on an objective basis has been left out. As the plot develops we see him as an individual struggling against Langton and Cardinal Pandulphus. He is given compassion and other human emotions, and this leads to the pathetic emphasis upon his death. Bale's conception of tragedy is quite hard to determine, and there is not a strong case for seeing the play as a complete example. Nevertheless Johan is presented as a victim, caught in a dilemma from which he cannot escape easily and which, as Bale sees it, involves overwhelming difficulties in carrying out his duty as a king. He is given several speeches which show the intensity of his suffering as a human being trying to carry out divine imperative:

> No prynce in the worlde   in suche captivyte
> As I am thys houre,   and all for ryghteousnesse. (ll. 2050–51)

However, he also has to encounter widow England and the Vice as Sedition, so that always his essence as a purely individualized character is placed in a context which challenges or extends it. Thus this characterization, though apparently realistic, acquires a special sense by association with characters of a different type, and through Johan's function in the play. The culmination of this process comes after Johan's death when Imperial Majesty is introduced as a kind of descendant in Bale's own times. This new character (not in the A text, as far as can be ascertained) takes over some of Johan's prestige in the plot, but also acts as a kind of restored king who administers justice and acts in the interest of his kingdom as Johan had essayed to do.

Possibly this characterization, together with that of Veritas, was suggested by *Pammachius*, the Latin eschatological drama by Thomas

Kirchmeyer, printed at Wittenberg in May 1538, which Bale translated at about this time. Like *King Johan*, Kirchmeyer's play shows a shift near the end, from the historical past to a contemporary setting. The character is made more complex, as Imperial Majesty seems to be a version, idealized and deferential, of Henry VIII himself. Here again we must regret that we do not know what he looked like on stage, or how he conducted himself, but there are many ways in which he might have been made to suggest an identification with the king. It would be a delicate matter, but a good deal would depend upon its success. Identification is made likely by his entering line, which refers to "our predecessours" (l. 2322), and to the emphasis given by Veritas to the issue of royal supremacy: "a kynge is judge over all / By Gods appoyntment," and also by more direct verbal resonance:

> I charge yow therfor,   as God hath charged me,
> To gyve to your kynge   hys due supremyte.[10]

Civil Order's prompting—"Of the Christen faythe   playe now the true defendar" (l. 2427)—may be a reference to Henry's title, Defensor Fidei, bestowed by the papacy in 1521, but now used by Bale with a different twist. It seems certain that Bale could not actually bring a character called Henry VIII into his play—the risks would have been too great—but the possibility of oblique reference to the king gives point to the theory that Bale was deeply concerned to bring influence to bear upon him. If, as noted above, one performance did take place in the presence of Cranmer, the pressure on the occasion would have been remarkable.

Thematically, Sedition is at the heart of the moral action of the play. Generated perhaps by a patriotic sentiment observable in much of Bale's work, dramatic and otherwise, he is a threat to the Protestant cause because he undermines the Protestant nation, bringing in foreign and popish conspiracy. But Bale's theatrical gift led him to make much of this part. Sedition is present in most of the scenes, and he has a specific direction in the plot: he ridicules England, leads the estates characters astray, takes part in the stage show with the Pope, enacts the historical role of Stephen Langton, aids Dissimulation in farcical episodes at the poisoning of the king, and finally is punished for his misdeeds. The role requires a versatile actor, who can take a large onstage responsibility; he must be quick with words, must have a comic presence, must possess the physical mobility needed to take part in stage devices, must be able to sing in groups and solo, must be able to

make rapid costume changes and to manipulate aliases. The part is rich
in certain distinct stage manners such as laughing and weeping, and in
many verbal games such as playing upon words (see below). Though
like Infidelity in *Three Laws*, he is not so called, he is an early example
of the conventional vice. Possibly the name, and indeed the role, had
not acquired the popularity which was to come in interludes after about
1550. Bale seems to make a significant contribution to the development of the convention in both moral and theatrical aspects. The only
known previous exponent of comparable importance is John Heywood,
who does call both Merry Report in *Wether* and Neither Loving nor
Loved in *Love* "the Vice"; but Heywood's characters are not embodi-
ments of evil, and his plays do not follow the conventions of moral alle-
gories. Bale's enhancement of the staginess of the role in revision
increases the probability that he saw great scope in it. There is no doubt
that this ubiquitous and versatile part makes a splendid theatrical contrast with the serious and quasi-tragical Johan.

On the moral plane, Sedition is the central evil, a focus and an inspi-
ration for the other evils, and his ubiquity makes a significant moral
impact. He is not a devil, but there is something distinctly devilish about
his ingenious destructiveness and his lack of humanity. His close attention to the audience and to the impact he is making adds to this:

> Godes blyssyng have ye!   This ger than wyll worke I trust. (l. 1271)

Having gone off to change his costume he comes on with:

> Have in onys ageyne,   in spyght of all myn enymyes. (l. 627)

However engaging he may be to the audience, he has still to be rejected
at the end, and in the last sequence, as Imperial Majesty closes in on him,
his comic attempt at evasion puts him on the wrong side:

> Some man tell the Pope   I besyche ye with all my harte,
> How I am ordered   for takynge the Churches parte,
> That I may be put   in the Holye Letanye
> With Thomas Beckett,   for I thynke I am as wurthye.
> Praye to me with candels   for I am a saynt alreadye.
> O blessed Saynt Partryck,   I see the, I, verylye! (ll. 2587–92)

Bale knows very well how to use this character; he has extended his
effectiveness considerably beyond that of Infidelity.

Language and Verse

The two most significant influences upon Bale's language in *King Johan* are religious ones, both Protestant and Catholic, and the theatrical conventions of villainy show themselves most clearly in the vice. The Protestant influence is strongest in the language of the Bible, and in the vocabulary of comment upon it, especially Tyndale's. Johan's part, with its preaching role, is remarkably economical in imagery, and it seems that Bale may have been essaying a plain style for him. There is less sign of classical learning in this play than in *Three Laws*. There is, however, occasional imagery:

> Nobylyte also   whych ought hys prynce to assyste
> Is vanyshed awaye   as it were a wynter myste. (ll. 1540–41)
> Lyke backes, in the darke   ye alweys take yowre flyght,   [*bats*]
> Flytteryng in fanseys,   and ever abhorre the lyght. (ll. 365–66)

Some of it traceable to the poetry of the Bible:

> Owre pristes are rysyn   throwgh lyberte of kynges
> By ryches to pryd   and other unlawfull doynges. (ll. 1516–17)

There is also a theatrical use of the language of the liturgy, especially Latin, which is used to direct sympathy toward Johan. Thus, for his submission to the Cardinal, he speaks in Latin.

That Sedition should be the star of the show in theatrical terms conforms with Bale's suspicion that theatrical devices were inclined to be evil deceptions. To this effect he heaps linguistic devices into the parts of Sedition and his associates. This shows itself in all manner of word play, including puns, verbal abuse, slips of the tongue, proverbs,[11] and sexual and scatological jokes. A typical example is the slip of the tongue which is a common feature of the word games of vices before and after Sedition:

> I have a great mynd   to be a lecherous man—
> A wengonce take yt—   I wold saye a relygyous man. (ll. 304–05)

Such a device is part of the recognition features of the vice. When a group of vices is onstage together there are many examples of distorting language for comic but also evil effect:

Usurpid Power:	But tell me one thyng: dost thow not preche the Gospell?
Dissymulacyon:	No, I promyse yow, I defye yt to the devyll of hell!
Usurpid Power:	Yf I knewe thow dedyst thow shuldest have non absolucyon.
Dissymulacyon:	Yf I do, abjure me or put me to execucyon.
Privat Welth:	I dare say he brekyth no popyshe constytucyon.
Usurpid Power:	Soche men are worthy to have owre contrybucyon: I assoyle the here, behynde and also beforne.

(ll. 855–61: a scatological pun?)

These characters also use scraps from the liturgy, thus identifying their papist support but also distorting them by parody and so discrediting the liturgy:

Pater noster, I pray God   bryng hym sone to his grave;
Qui es in celis,   with an vengeable *sanctyficetur*,'
Or elles Holy Chyrche   shall never thryve, by Saynt Peter.   (ll. 643–45)

Compared to *Three Laws,* this play relies more upon couplets and less upon rime couée. This may be a reflection of a substantial difference of dramatic pace and texture, and of the nature of what is enacted on the stage. The former play has more time given to the extended speeches of self-explanation and less to rapid dialogue with other characters. For this purpose, couplets work very well, especially as Bale's use of the caesura helps with the speed of expression:

Sedycyon:	I marvele greatly where Dissymulacyon is.
Dissymylacyon:	I wyll come anon, if thu tarry tyll I pysse.
Sedycyon:	I beshrewe your hart! Where have ye bene so longe?
Dissymulacyon:	In the gardene, man, the herbes and wedes amonge, And there have I gote the poyson of a toade.

(ll. 2006–2010)

This passage illustrates Bale's commonest choice of line length. His system depends upon five stresses with the caesura following two accented syllables. After the caesura there are usually three accented syllables. We have noted that Bale intervened many times in A's text to mark this caesura and on some occasions moved it, to divide the line according to his desired rhythm. Adams (51) cites the line:

By the messe and that   is not worth a rottyn wardon. (l. 971)   [*pear*]

in which the caesura has been shifted from its place in the A text after
"not." Although Bale is very consistent in his count of five stresses, he
tolerates considerable variation in the number of unstressed syllables,
which helps to vary the speed of much of his dialogue. The reflection or
expansion of meaning in the second part of the line in relation to the first
half is also a key feature, and one which is present in his other main verse
form, rime royal.

Bale uses this stanzaic form in a manner reminiscent of *Three Laws*,
essentially for the most weighty parts of the play. In this he follows a
well-established convention of morality plays. Here it is used especially
for characters concerned with the exposition of doctrine, such as the
Interpretour in his division of the play into two acts, and Veritas in his
final settlement, in which the estates characters follow suit. The stanzaic
form also appears in Johan's introductory speech and in the crucial
speech when he is dying. In the latter, as he addresses his subjects, the
elevated diction is matched by a rhetorical dignity and a firm rhythm:

> Farwell, noble men,   with the clergye spirytuall;
> Farwell, men of lawe,   with the whole commynnalte.
> Your disobedyence   I do forgyve yow all
> And desyre God   to perdon your iniquyte.
> Farwell, swete Englande,   now last of all to the;
> I am ryght sorye   I coulde do for the nomore,
> Farwele ones agayne,   yea, farwell for evermore. (ll. 2174–80)

There are, however, interesting variations on this policy. Rime royal is
also used for one expository speech by Civil Order and one by Usurped
Power (ll. 381–94 and 948–54); and Dissimulation, near the end of the
first act, describes at greater length the coming activities of Usurped
Power, who is about to call the Lateran Council. For Bale this was a climactic moment in the medieval papacy's campaign against heretics and
pagans (ll. 984–1025).

Religion and Politics

If we draw together the evidence already discussed about the dating of
the two versions of the play, we can work on the assumption that the A
text was copied after May 1538, probably with a performance in mind,

either before or after the copy was made. The rediscovered, rejected sheets show that Bale incorporated virtually everything from the A text into the B text. It is therefore possible to argue, conversely, that much of the ending of the B text, beyond the point where it can be checked, also includes substantially the original ending. In other words, although there is evidence of additions and changes of emphasis, the outline of the play may not have changed much, and there is a high probability that many of the attitudes embodied in the A text inform the later version.

Such a reading of the complete text means that most of the play might reflect Bale's state of mind around the second half of 1538, just about the time when there is circumstantial evidence for two Cromwell-backed performances. A consideration of the political and religious targets embedded in the play matches this assumption remarkably well. Bale aimed to encourage patriotic resistance to external religious and military pressure; he criticized the estates, especially the Nobility and the Clergy, for disloyalty to the king (Johan standing for Henry); he ridiculed many of the customs and practices of the Catholic Church; he wanted to promote the Gospel; and perhaps most important, but also most difficult to achieve, he wanted to nudge or persuade Henry to go further along the way towards Bale's own brand of Protestantism, bearing in mind that Henry was rarely consistent in the religious changes and that he acted sometimes from personal caprice as well as from a spirit of opportunism. It is also significant that this reading of the current situation and the objectives set out were substantially those of Cromwell who was obviously in a position to be intimately and comprehensively informed of the state of the nation at this time.

Events from 1536 to 1539 may throw some light on this.[12] The Bill for the Suppression of the Monasteries was introduced by Henry himself to Parliament in 1536. At about the same time, an attempt to codify changes toward Protestantism was made in the Ten Articles, which were followed by Cromwell's first set of Injunctions. In the following year a committee of bishops produced, without direct input from Henry, *The Institution of a Christian Man,* known as the *Bishops' Book.* Once this was out, Henry set about annotating it in ways which recalled Catholic practice: in particular he supported auricular confession, a key subject in *King Johan* as a means by which Sedition acquires information and sets up initiatives. The king's religious caution here may well have been related to the exigencies of external affairs, for there was a significant threat of a foreign invasion arising from an alliance between Francis I of France and the Emperor Charles V. This became more real after two meetings and a

10-year truce between them in the summer of 1538.[13] If England were
to be isolated in Europe, it became important for Henry not to be seen
as leading a radical Protestant nation. This issue may of course have fit-
ted in with his own personal religious preferences, but it is clear that
Cromwell was engaged in strengthening the links with Protestant
Europe, symbolized perhaps by the negotiations over the proposed marriage with Anne of Cleves, a Protestant; the beginnings of this development occurred in June 1538.[14]

Perhaps because of the external threat which led to a vigorous policy
of military preparation, some of the nobility saw an opportunity for
power play, the outcome of which was a group of executions, including
that of the Marquis of Exeter in November 1538. Instead of conspiring
in this way, Bale thought it might have been better to be loyal to the
crown. However, the religious position remained unstable, and it must
have been felt by many Protestants that there was still much to hope for
and to fear. In September Cromwell's second set of Injunctions required
the placing of an English Bible in every parish church. It is clear that
Henry was very nervous about this as a potential source of instability
and strife. The cult of St. Thomas à Becket was suppressed also in
November, but at about the same time Henry himself intervened personally in the interrogation of John Lambert, who was burned for his
views against transubstantiation on 22 November.[15] Shortly afterward,
the pope issued the Bull of Excommunication against Henry on 17
December 1538. Though there were many Protestant enthusiasts who
supported the changes that were coming about, it is also apparent that
there were very many people who resented these changes and looked
back to the relative security of late medieval Catholic England.

King Johan is redolent with many of the issues summarized here. We
can see particularly the emphasis upon the royal supremacy and Bale's
acute sense that the religious welfare of the people is the direct, God-
given responsibility of a king—something that Bale wished to underline
in a time of tension. At the end of the play, Sedition is defeated and the
values of the Gospel religion are asserted. If by any chance Bale or
Cromwell hoped for an audience which contained the king, it was essential that the monarch should not be challenged over issues about which
he was known to be adamant, such as transubstantiation, which Bale
rejected, but which appears nowhere in the play. If the audience did not
include the king there were still plenty of risks. This may very well
account for the intensity of the comedy surrounding the disgraceful and
disloyal activities of the Vice and his associates, for the best way of deal-

ing with them might be to laugh them out of court. Such an interpretation of the context of the play draws attention to the remarkable dramatic expertise Bale was able to deploy in pursuance of political objectives.

It is as well to bear in mind that if Bale's primary strategy in *King Johan* may have been to bring persuasion on the King, there was still much to hope for. It is thus ironic that the horse may already have bolted, for there is a distinct possibility that the countermovement had begun in the autumn of 1538.[16] Perhaps the political exigencies changed, and perhaps the king was not to be persuaded. The play may have been performed in September 1538 and January 1539, but by the next May the Six Articles, which effectively put a stop to most of the changes that advanced the Protestant cause, were in Parliament. Even though tactically Cromwell may have supported or accepted the views embodied in these measures, it was perhaps the beginning of the end for him, and his fall in turn led to Bale's first exile in 1540.

In this complex political situation the play reflects a remarkable variety of important topical issues. Bale shows great capacity in his systematic inclusion of so many in his text. Moreover, the revised text is very consistent, showing that Bale had a firm grasp of this subject matter. His achievement as a dramatist is that his play, working toward these objectives, is expressed in a form that is technically very skilled. The variety of his theatrical texture, ranging from the quasi-tragedy of Johan's isolation and death to the comic fecundity of the vices, might make it a success on stage as well as a politically acute document. The highly original manipulation of allegorical and historical spheres of reference makes a special impact. The missing element is how his performance skills would have enhanced the text, but the richness of this text in dramatic terms suggests that it would have been very effective. A minute number of surviving contemporary reports suggest that the play did make its point in performance. On 11 January 1539 Cranmer sent Cromwell a transcript of a deposition by Thomas Browne of Shawlteclyf in Kent, noting:

> This deponent tolde that he hadde bene at my Lorde of Canterbury's, and there hadd harde [heard] one of the beste matiers that he ever saw, towching King John; and than sayd that he had harde divers tymes preistes and clerkes say that King John did loke like one that hadd run frome brynnyng [burning] of a house, butt this deponent knewe now that yt was nothing treu; for as farr as he perceyved King John was as noble a prince as ever was in England; and therby we myght perceyve

that he was begynner of the puttyng down of the Bisshop of Rome, and therof we myght be all gladd.[17]

Whether this disposition spelled triumph or disaster for Bale in real life is another matter. The balance of evidence is that the political forces he was seeking to master were too much for him, in spite of his dramatic skills.

In some respects the B text pulls away from the concerns of 1538–39, particularly as the extensions to Johan's part concerning his pathetic death may not be readily applied to Henry. This change in emphasis may be part of an intention to give the play some independence from its original context. It reminds us that, even with a political intention as sharp as Bale's, there may still be artistic considerations inherent in the work itself. Even though the extensions to Sedition's part are in line with Bale's original puposes, they may also have been made because of theatrical considerations.

Chapter Six
The Biblical Plays

Text

The full titles of John Bale's three extant biblical plays draw attention to his thinking about kinds of drama as well as to his doctrinal intentions:

A Tragedye or Enterlude manyfestyng the Chefe Promyses of God unto Man by All Ages in the Olde Lawe, from the Fall of Adam to the Incarnacyon of the Lorde Jesus Christ (God's Promises)

A Brefe Comedy or Enterlude of Johan Baptystes Preachynge in the Wyldernesse, openynge the Craftye Assaultes of the Hypocrytes, with the Gloryouse Baptyme of the Lorde Jesus Christ (John Baptist's Preaching)

A Brefe Comedy or Enterlude concernynge The Temptacyon of our Lorde and Saver Jesus Christ by Sathan in the Desart (The Temptation)

The title pages of the earliest copies, which were printed in 1547 or 1548, claim that they were compiled in 1538, but they appear only in the second phase of Bale's play lists, that published in the *Summarium* and later. This leaves us with a number of puzzles which cannot easily be solved. On the one hand, these biblical plays, though they heartily embody the new Protestant doctrines, do not set forth their ideas in quite such an adversarial way as *Three Laws* and *King Johan*, and they make their points in a much less humorous and less strikingly versatile theatrical manner. They are also much shorter than Bale's other two plays, even though they treat the chosen episodes more fully than do the Corpus Christi cycles. But this is not to suggest that they are not effectively written for the stage. They are remarkable for their different approaches to biblical material in terms of structure and design.

There is no doubt that the three plays listed in the *Summarium* are the same as the extant plays, in that the Latin incipits given there are close translations of the first lines of each play as printed. The presumption must be that they are later than *Three Laws* and *King Johan*, and we must suppose that, if this is so, Bale extensively rethought his dramatic method. As we shall see, this may well have been the result of a desire to create a substitute for the traditional cycle plays which had been developing since about the year 1375 in a number of English cities, and which were still being performed *in extenso*.

The presentation of the printed texts is very similar, all three being attributed on the basis of type to Dirik van der Straten who brought out a number of Protestant works at his press in Wesel. *God's Promises* appeared separately, but the other two were printed with continuous page signatures. However, the original of *John Baptist's Preaching* has been lost, perhaps because it was detached from its companion, *Temptation,* at the distribution of the Harley library in the eighteenth century. Fortunately, it was reprinted for *The Harleian Miscellany* in 1744, an edition which is now the sole authority for the text. Although it embodies some modifications to fit with contemporary expectations, it is clear that the lost original was the companion of *The Temptation*, and many of the linguistic features of its exemplar have survived.

Although there are a significant number of stage directions in the texts, they are not comprehensive. As they are all in Latin, it is possible that they were primarily included with readers rather than performers in mind, though this is not conclusive. They certainly draw attention to parts of the plays where it is necessary to envisage action on stage. In *John Baptist's Preaching* three characters, Turba Vulgaris, Publicanus, and Miles Armatus, are each baptized by John: although this is quite clear in the dialogue, the stage directions point specifically to the exact moment, as in:

> *Hunc tunc baptisat Joannes flectentem genua.* (l. 120 s.d.; "Then John baptizes him (Turba Vulgaris) as he bends his knee.")

Similar instructions, not identically worded, are provided for the other two. Later Sadducaeus and Pharisaeus speak, in an aside, to each other; this is marked by the direction *Invicem alloquuntur* (l. 206 s.d.; "They speak together privately.").

There are similar instances in *God's Promises*, but here Bale may be stressing a formal symmetry in print. The play is arranged into seven acts: in each, an Old Testament character receives God's promise and celebrates it by initiating the singing of an anthem. At the point in each act where the singing begins, there is a full stage direction (which could not be deduced from the dialogue), such as:

> *Tunc sonora voce, provolutis genibus, Antiphonam incipit, O Sapientia, quam prosequetur chorus, cum organis, eo interum exeunte. Vel sub eodem tono poterit sic Anglice cantari* (l. 178 s.d.; "Then on bended knee he begins in a loud

voice the anthem, O Wisdom, which the Chorus takes up, with an organ
accompaniment, as he goes out. Or with the same accompaniment it
could be sung in English, thus." Bale's translations for each antiphon
make the point that he advocated worship in English.)

This stage direction gives information about the liturgy to accompany
the performance, about the kind of musical accompaniment, and about
the way the music fits into the movement on stage. The fact that there
are closely similar instructions near the end of each of the other six acts
(not worded exactly the same) makes it clear that Bale envisaged this
procedure in some detail and wanted his readers to be aware of it. We
shall return later to the significance of the music chosen.

Bale's underlying decision to print these texts in 1547 or 1548 may
be associated with the anticipated death of King Henry and its after-
math; he no doubt hoped that they would help to establish his position
in the new Protestant state. This assumption may be supported by his
titling, which recalls classical dramatic modes, even though in the structure of the texts such an intention is not carried out with marked attention to the classical practices that were then becoming more widely
known.

How the original versions of 1538 relate to these later printed texts is
a matter of conjecture. If Bale was active as the leader of a troupe of performers in the 1530s, it is notable that these plays would require smaller
casts than the other two. *God's Promises* could be done by two actors,
supported by singers; *Temptation* could also be managed by two actors
with very little support from two more for the small parts for Angels;
John Baptist's Preaching is plotted for four actors working closely together.
This suggests that originally they were not conceived to meet the same
requirements as the two longer plays. Such a difference is supported by
a number of aspects in the dramatic mode of these plays, as we shall see.

Plot

Although Bale was apparently working on material similar to that in the
Corpus Christi cycles, he brings different assumptions to his work and he
also addresses the opportunity of playwriting in very different ways in
each of the three biblical plays. The symmetry of the seven-act structure
in *God's Promises* is its most striking feature. This no doubt accords with
Bale's practice, notable elsewhere, of creating structural patterns in his
plots. We have already noted this in *Three Laws*, but here the plot is

much more strictly arranged. Each of the Old Testament heroes (Adam, Noah, Moses, Abraham, David, and Isaiah) is given the opportunity of confessing his faults, but also of asking for mercy for himself and for other sinners of his time.[1] In each act Pater Coelestis complains about human wickedness, often giving a list of human offences, but he eventually admits mercy and gives an appropriate sign of the renewed promise. The hero then initiates the singing of an anthem which terminates the act. The last act, devoted to John Baptist, brings the sequence to an end at Advent, thereby suggesting that this might have been conceived as a seasonal play. The anthems chosen are all part of the preparation for Advent, and are drawn from the traditional liturgy in the form of the "Great O's," antiphons sung in the week before Christmas.

In strict terms there is no story and no plot to be developed, but Bale does rely on the outline of biblical history to Advent: his intention is more emblematic. Indeed, many biblical stories and incidents are adduced, such as David and Bersabe (Bathsheba), and the plagues of Egypt. Hence the play works partly by a consciousness of scriptural history, even though the structure is not strictly a narrative. This is a noteworthy dramatic achievement, and it should be seen in relation to Bale's managing of the traditional narrative material of the Corpus Christi plays. We must assume that Bale was aware of these, for he would have been in the vicinity of performances at Norwich, Ipswich, Beverley, Doncaster, Wakefield, and York at various times, and the emphasis in these performances upon aspects of Catholic doctrine (particularly things like the cult of the Virgin, hagiology, and miracles) would have seemed inappropriate to him. Instead he is manifestly interested in the teaching of the Gospel and in the promotion of the doctrine of justification by faith. For Bale, scriptural history worked differently from its traditional function in the cycles. Although he does use some of the figural links, his real concern is with the promises and the new Protestant contract between God and man, with an emphasis upon the latter as an individual.

Because the promises of God are a leading motif, each of the episodes is tailored to reflect them. Thus the popular story of Abraham and Isaac is omitted in favor of a concentration upon Abraham as the father of a nation. The presence of Baleus Prolocutor in each of these biblical plays allows Bale to give a particular twist to the structure in each case. There remains, however, an interesting tension in *God's Promises* in that the urge to preach embodied in the Prolocutor's part is mixed with an intention to worship in the seven anthems. As it happens, the play was performed again at Kilkenny in 1553, and since Bale's account of the

performance refers to an organ and to singing, it seems likely that this
liturgical element was still included. Probably Bale wished not only to
fashion the scriptural treatment of the cycle plays but also to include an
element of worship which could be different in spirit from what he
objected to in the establishment versions. It should be remembered that
the Corpus Christi plays still retained much of their traditional reputation when Bale first wrote *God's Promises*, and that there was to be a
revival of them in Mary's reign. Bale shows remarkable originality in the
plot of this play. He brings together some traditional material related to
the prophecies about Christ (found in exegetical writings and in the
Corpus Christi plays; all the characters Bale uses can be found at various
places in the cycles), the leading Protestant doctrine of the promises, and
the elegant feature of the Advent antiphons (with which he would have
been familiar in his Carmelite years, but which probably still appealed to
him because they are scriptural in origin).

The plots of the other two biblical plays are much more influenced by
the scriptural narrative, but Bale has to ensure that a new interpretation
of the role of scripture is promulgated in them. Once again he pursues a
softer line than in *Three Laws* and *King Johan*. For *The Temptation* the original model in Matthew gave a closely interlocking dialogue between
Christ and Satan which is inherently dramatic in that the speeches react
sharply to one another.[2] Similarly, the three temptations offer a repetitive
structure in which parallels can be offered between them. These temptations take place in three different locations—the desert, the pinnacle of
the temple, and the mountain—each appropriate to the temptation
involved. There is also the archetypal conflict between good and evil figures, which can be resolved by the comedic triumph of Christ. Bale followed the traditional interpretation which was added to scripture by
such exegetists as Ludolphus the Carthusian. This interpretation included the ideas that Christ's humanity was a divine instrument, and that by
enduring the 40 days in the wilderness, Christ submitted to the Old
Law—a submission which was necessary if he was to increase the Devil's
doubt as to whether he was god or man.

Two changes made by Bale in the traditional interpretation make
clear that he was interested in a new reading of the narrative. These
changes can partly be traced in the work of other Protestant writers such
as Luther and Calvin. One is the danger that Satan could beguile Christ
into mistrusting God; hence Bale has Christ describe Satan's proposition
of the miraculous conversion of the bread as "unnecessarye." Similarly,
there had to be a readjustment about Christ's fasting, which was

undoubtedly scriptural and could not therefore be ignored, even though fasting was not popular among Protestants. It could, however, be presented that fasting was not meant to be imitated by man, but that by the act of fasting Christ should transport all men to admire him:

> Thynke not me to fast bycause I wolde yow to fast,
> For than ye thynke wronge and have vayne judgement.
>   (*The Temptation*, ll. 44–45)

In addition, Christ presents his fasting as a means of provoking Satan, an echo of the traditional divine deception of the Devil. This was a traditional preoccupation of Temptation plays following the so-called theory of the "abuse of power," whereby Satan's attempt to kill Christ in the belief that he was only a man revealed that he was exceeding his allowed function.[3]

The argument over the the interpretation of the scripture adduced by Satan also attracts Bale's dramatic, as well as theological, interest. According to Matthew, the Devil did cite Deuteronomy, but Bale shows in the dialogue that the quotation is incomplete, and that by the omission of four words, Satan sought to mislead Christ:

Satan Tentator: Well than, I sayd true, and as it lyeth in the text.

Jesus Christus: Yea, but ye omytted foure wordes whych foloweth next,
                      As "in all thy wayes," whych if ye put out of syght,
                      Ye shall never take that place of scripture a ryght.

                                                        (ll. 225–28)

Bale's development of plot in *John Baptist's Preaching* has less scriptural narrative, and indeed the narrative he embodies is only a part of the action. He makes much use of John Baptist's active preaching role, using details of scriptural imagery and inventing an audience from the account of St. Luke. As we have seen elsewhere, Bale attributed heroic proportions to the role of the preacher, and it is not surprising that here John Baptist is much developed in this respect. Bale had a special interest in the Baptist, originating presumably in his studies of the Carmelite order, and he lists one of his lost plays as a *Life of John the Baptist*, in 14 books, which does not seem to correspond to the extant play.

The first part of the play shows how the Baptist ministers to many different sinners, and how he can preach to different social levels:

The symple fysher shall now be notable;
The spirytuall Pharyse a wretche detestable.
(*John Baptist's Preaching*, ll. 78–79)

Mixed with this is an attack on the Seven Deadly Sins (ll. 88–95). Then, after their confessions, he baptizes the three representatives of society whom Bale creates from brief mentions as common nouns in the Vulgate (Luke 3:10–14): Miles Armatus (armed soldier), Turba Vulgaris (the common crowd), and Publicanus (the tax collector). We also find further exploration of the Law in that the Baptist emphasizes the New Law, and vigorously attacks legalistic aspects of the old religion as embodied in the characters of Pharisaeus and Sadducaeus. Here the conflict between the preacher and the priests, who are merely legalistic, is marked by John's outrage:

You boast yourselves moch of ryghteousnesse and scyence,
And yet non more vyle nor fuller of neglygence.
How can ye escape the vengeance that is commynge
Upon the unfaythfull whych wyll admytt no warnynge? (ll. 261–64)

The narrative is completed by the baptism of Christ, which is played so as to show Christ's submission to holy discipline. The emphasis found in the cycles upon ritualistic and sacramental aspects of baptism as one of the seven sacraments is avoided by Bale, but he does show the descent of the Holy Spirit in the form of a dove (as noted in a stage direction at l. 431). Such a decision about staging suggests that Bale was interested in symbolic acts on stage, and this is borne out in some of his other plays. A new spiritual baptism is now envisaged as the Baptist rejoices over what are Protestant themes:

I geve but water; the sprete, Lorde, thu dost brynge. (l. 391)

Character

The types of characters Bale uses are related to the biblical sources of these plays in as much as they are often named after scriptural persons; but as the mode of the plays is different from the largely human convention of the Corpus Christi plays, there is room for characterization which is abstract or even based upon types. Moreover, both the poetic and the artistic aims of the plays affect how the characters are handled; and there is also influence from the didactic aims which Bale set for himself.

We have noted in discussing *King Johan* that, although Johan is a historical character presented with a degree of realism, his nature has apparently been modified by Bale, and that he also comes into contact with characters who are not partially or entirely historical but rather are determined by abstract considerations. A similar dramatic context is also important in the biblical plays. The selection of characters in *God's Promises*, for example, is made on a chronological basis, but each character is given an epithet, which appears in all his speech headings, to bring out his inherent virtue. In spite of the wrongdoings which they each confess, Bale thus wishes to show them as heroic. David is Rex Pius; Abraham is Fidelis; Moses, Sanctus; and Noah, Justus. For Adam his humanity is stressed as well as his anticipation of Christ in that he is called Primus Homo. Esaias is given the prestigious title Propheta.

Temptation provides an opportunity for confrontation between two familiar characters, Christ and Satan. Here and elsewhere in the biblical plays, a great deal depends upon the identification of traditional historical or legendary characters. For Bale, of course, legend and history were much closer than they would be considered in modern times. An awareness of the power of the past with its traditional attributes informs the characters in these plays. Always there is a sense that the biblical narrative is responsible for the nature of the characters as Bale presents them. It is probably this above all which gives to these characters a sufficient impression of individuality; they operate for the audience within a known historical context. With Christ and Satan, in fact, Bale works to achieve a sharp differentiation—the same traditional differentiation that appeared in the earlier mystery plays, and that was reinforced by iconographic convention. Bale's Christ is emphatically human, having suffered and wanting to preserve his humanity, partly as a cloak to conceal his divinity. Nevertheless, he has heroic attributes based upon scripture:

> For God hath promysed that hys shall treade the dragon
> Underneth their fete, with the fearce roarynge lyon.
> *(The Temptation,* ll. 349–50)

By contrast, Satan is guileful and articulate. Although his various ploys are easily defeated by Christ, he is not a ridiculous character. Both characters are given opening soliloquies, and it is notable that neither addresses the audience; rather, both speak as though consulting with themselves. Satan particularly mixes self-address, in which he works out his moves, with ostensibly sympathetic attempts to help Christ. In this respect Bale's method of handling character is in line with medieval practice in both Corpus Christi plays and moralities.

A key dramatic feature of Bale's characterization arises in his presentation of dramatic conflict between characters. Bale was always sharply aware that this could be one of the strongest features of drama, and it gives force to much of his dialogue. Although in the biblical plays he carefully avoids comic contrast of characters, there is nevertheless a strong sense of oppositional writing as between them. The conflict between Christ and Satan in *The Temptation* shows Christ waiting to expose the wickedness and confusion of Satan in an uncompromising way. In comparison with the versions in the Corpus Christi cycles, Bale has developed both roles extensively: Christ to show his sense of human obligation in a divine context, and Satan to show the elaborate attempt to demean Christ, and in particular to trap him through the misuse of scripture.

Presentation of the divinity was a somewhat difficult task for a Protestant playwright, in view of the necessity to avoid idolatry. By making Christ human, but human under the requirements of the Law, the difficulty is partly obviated. Similarly, in the creation of Pater Coelestis in *God's Promises*, Bale concentrates upon the supreme wrath of God, which might be seen as a legitimate and distancing attribute of divinity. As we have seen, the structure of this play clarifies this, since in each act the human characters are seen as representatives of a corrupt humanity deserving the just rebuke from God. The plagues of Egypt are very appropriate to this concept (ll. 457–63). To this may be added the bitter passage in which Abraham barters with God to establish how many just men must be found if his wrath is to be averted. It is not surprising too that this episode, working downward from 50 just men to 45, 40, 30, 20, and ultimately 10, is derived exactly and in detail from scripture.[4] It is only as the coming of Christ approaches in the sixth act that God is less vengeful, with the messianic hope expressed by Isaiah.

It is a feature of *God's Promises*, however, that the conflict is worked between the wrath of God and the pleas of men. There are no villains other than the inherent wickedness of mankind. Perhaps it is here that we may find some explanation for Bale's calling the play a tragedy. In spite of the uplifting ending, which rests upon the certainty of the promises of God, the play gives a very bleak picture of human failings and divine severity throughout the period of Old Testament history. For *John Baptist's Preaching* Bale sets up both the opposition of justice against human wrongdoing and the conflict of good and bad characters. Human guilt is expressed through the weaknesses of Turba Vulgaris, Publicanus, and Miles Armatus. Respectively, these are shown to be deficient in their practice of superstition (ll. 127–31), the danger of exploiting the poor (ll. 158–62), and the misuse of violence in war (ll. 177–81; but violence can be justified by God if the cause is right.). The action of the play shows that these characters are capable of salvation if they appreciate their role in the the Christian kingdom correctly. As with Nobility in *King Johan*, it is the real-life counterparts of these characters Bale sought to influence.

When it comes to Pharisaeus and Sadducaeus—again both are characters who represent generalized types—there is no way out, no real hope of change. Both show crafty villainy and a determination to dissemble in an attempt to undermine the Baptist. Like many evil characters they make their intention to deceive quite plain to the audience:

> Lete us dyssemble to understande hys meanynge . . .
> we must be sumwhat craftye . . .
> thu shalt se me undermynde hym very fynelye.
> (*John Baptist's Preaching*, ll. 208–12)

For Bale these characters are also representative of the evils of his own time, so that the use of traditional characters for whom parallels might be found in the traditional cycles is actually designed to bring out an allegorical resonance with a contemporary political issue. In their unspiritual application of the Law they stand for the corruption of the priesthood against which Luther and Bale fought intensely, and which undoubtedly Bale, at least, considered irremediable. Their ultimate position is that they set out to prevent John from preaching, and the parting shot is their fear that he will cause a political revolt:

> If we do not se for thys gere a dyrreccyon,
> This fellawe is lyke to make an insurreccyon;
> For to hys newe lernynge an infynyte cumpanye
> Of worldly rascalles come hyther suspycyouslye. (ll. 314–17)

It is perhaps significant that the matter of unrest is not in fact resolved, as though Bale felt it necessary or desirable to leave it open to question. One might add, though, that these two evil persons have another function, for their intervention also helps to define John's purpose and his growing awareness of his own destiny.

The use of the character Baleus Prolocutor in each of these plays has several functions, but it should be noted that the appearance of such overtly theological apologists was a feature of some traditional cycles, as seen in the Expositor figure in certain Chester plays. For Bale the need to explain, so as to bring out significant points of Protestant doctrine, and also the need to conclude with the correct emphasis, are clearly of polemical value. What is said is very much a kind of sermon, with frequent address to the "most Christen audyence." This included exhortation, such as, "For assaultes of Sathan lerne here the remedye" (*The Temptation*, l. 29). There is also a sense that this is a dramatic performance as well as a homiletic matter. There are occasional links to the other plays, and also a metatheatrical invitation to participate in the play:

> Of thys herafter ye shall
> Perceyve more at large by the story as it fall. (*The Tempatation*, ll. 34–35)

It may thus be felt that the function of the Prolocutor is to serve a combination of religious and theatrical purposes; this function points directly to Bale's concept of the drama. His use of the Prolocutor fits in with a pervasive sense emanating from many aspects of his dramatic work that, although he is very keen about the theological commitment of what he writes, he is also persistently aware of the force of theatrical writing. It may well be felt, however, that this should not lead us to suppose that without the theological aspects Bale would have been a more successful dramatist. It is probably wiser to see his theatrical gift as an indestructable part of his religious vision.

Language and Verse

The versification of these works follows the conventions already noted in Bale's other plays. He uses rime royal extensively for the most solemn parts, including all the Prolocutor's speeches at the beginnings and ends of each, and most of those by Pater Coelestis. In *God's Promises* the formal and regular structure is supported by extensive use of this stanza: for example, as each act draws to a close, the human protagonist leads up to the antiphon in this verse form. The last of those spoken by Joannes Baptista catches the mood of excitement, and also apparently draws in the musical accompaniment and possibly the audience:

> Helpe me to geve thankes to that lorde evermore
> Whych am unto Christ a cryars voyce in the desart
> To prepare the pathes and hygh wayes hym before,

For hys delyght is on the poore symple hart.
That innocent lambe from soch wyll never depart
As wyll faythfullye receyve hym with good mynde.
Lete our voyce then sounde in some swete musycall kynde.
(*God's Promises*, ll. 936–42)

The antiphon "O clavis David" follows immediately. In *The Temptation* Satan is given three rime royal stanzas in his first speech (ll. 57–77). The choice may be justified, because Satan speaks the truth about himself as well as about Christ:

I hearde a great noyse in Jordane now of late,
Upon one Jesus, soundynge from heaven above:
'Thys is myne owne sonne whych hath withdrawne al hate,
And he that doth stande most hyghly in my love.'
(*The Temptation*, ll. 64–67)

In the same passage he announces his real intention, real for him and real for the audience:

I wyll not leave hym tyll I knowe what he ys. (l. 71)

But also the deception is made plain:

A godly pretence outwardly must I beare
Semynge relygyouse, devoute and sad in my geare. (ll. 74–75)

The other principal meter is five-stress couplets, the incidence of which varies somewhat between the plays. In *God's Promises* they appear briefly in the middle of each act when the human character speaks to God. Abraham's bargaining, mentioned above (ll. 365–77), is constructed so that the speakers have alternate lines, splitting each couplet, an effect which gives a genuinely interlocking dialogue:

Abraham Fidelis:	Paradventure there maye be thirty founde amonge them.
Pater Coelestis:	Maye I fynde thirty I wyll nothynge do unto them.
Abraham Fidelis:	I take upon me to moche, lorde, in thy syght?
Pater Coelestis:	No, no, good Abraham, for I knowe thy faythe is ryght.
Abraham Fidelis:	No lesse I suppose than twenty can it have?
Pater Coelestis:	Coulde I fynde twenty that cytie wolde I save.

(*God's Promises*, ll. 369–74)

Occasionally the couplets are extended to give trimeters or quatrains with the same rhyme.

Different deployment of these principal meters in the other two plays is perhaps related to Bale's perception that *God's Promises* is a tragedy. While rime royal does appear in the others, it is notable that the exchanges between the Baptist and other characters are largely in couplets, with fewer irregularities. In *The Temptation* the couplets are the predominant meter: they carry the whole of the play from Satan's first approach, through the three temptations, to the end of the angels' celebration (ll. 78–398). In these episodes Bale achieves a variety of dramatic pace as well as sharp dialogic interchange. The only passages in rime royal are the two introductory soliloquies, and the Prologue and the Epilogue of the Prolocutor.

Bale's strategy for language in these plays is largely a matter of using biblical echoes. The reason for this is no doubt ideological, especially in connection with the superior authority of the Bible, but the effect is that striking images often appear in the dialogue, as in the passage by Joannes Baptista which was quoted above. In *The Temptation* the scriptural source provides a series of speeches which Bale is careful to copy, particularly for the wording of each temptation. However, he adds his own Protestant gloss neatly where applicable:

Satan Tentator: Make of these stone breade,   and geve your bodye hys fode.

Jesus Christ: No offence is it   to eate whan men be hungrye;
                 But to make stones breade   *it is unnecessarye*.
                                       (ll. 105–6; my italics)

For the character of Satan, Bale may have had some particular dramatic precedents and objectives in respect to language. The characterization of a tempter was obviously one which had an extensive dramatic heritage. Bale shows a particular concern to differentiate Satan's language from Christ's, yet at the same time he is apparently not attempting to create a comic villain. In fact, he draws a fine line, avoiding ridicule and suggesting corruption and cunning. (In later interludes, such as Ulpian Fulwell's *Like Will to Like*, the Devil is a ridiculous grotesque.) The falseness of Satan's intention is shown in *The Temptation* by such words and phrases as "cooles to steare" (l. 70); "unsavery geare" (l. 124); "in scoff" (l. 197); "scath" (l. 213); "glose" (l. 218; a word which Bale may have found in Tyndale); and "pratlynge" (l. 267). All three of the plays considered in this chapter have few proverbs: Blatt lists only 12 altogether

(215). In dealing with proverbs, we must be aware that they can have many differing effects and that they cannot really be considered in isolation; it is context which often may suggest social level or dramatic intent. However, for Satan the tone of three proverbs fits in with his characterization as built up by his language: "for there ye touche fre holde" (l. 245); "not worth a torde" (l. 294); and "I . . . take thy wordes but as wynde" (l. 338). The sardonic dismissal of what Christ is saying is essential to Satan's character.

It is also to be noted that this character does operate as a tempter. The language of his part is concerned with persuading Christ to do wrong: many other evil characters embody evil rather than tempting, but here Bale is specifically interested in this function, which involves argument.

The touch of demotic speech appears again in the language of the Phariseus and Sadducaeus. We have already noted the strength of these characterizations, and their speech is effective in its combination of vigorous language with satirical intent by the author, conscious of the polemical issues:

> It become not the to shew what we shall do,
> We knowynge the lawe and the prophecyes also.
> Go teache thy olde shoes, lyke a busye pratlynge fole,
> For we wyll non be of thys newe fangeled scole.
> We are men lerned; we knowe the auncyent lawes
> Of our forefathers. Thy newes are not worth two strawes.
> (*John Baptist's Preaching*, ll. 273–78)

In summarizing, one might ask why Bale chose to write in verse. One obvious reason is the continuing convention that all his dramatic precedents were in verse. Beyond this convention, however, lies the power of verse forms to manage emphasis, to sharpen contrasting and parallel phrases as well as syntax and tone, to isolate concepts and images, and to strengthen interrelating diction and dialogue. His is not a slavish imitation of precedents but a way of finding a voice for powerful ideas. If Bale's versification is appreciated in this way, it reflects the high value he places upon it, as we noted in discussing the nondramatic works.

Religion and Politics

It seems likely from external evidence that Bale was intending to present his three printed biblical plays—*God's Promises, John Baptist's Preaching,* and *The Temptation*—as reflecting a coherent purpose which in its dra-

matic intention offers a view of history, and which concentrates upon the
life of Christ. To an extent this purpose may be a reaction against some
of the material in the Corpus Christi cycles, such as the episodes in the *N
Town* cycle which elaborate the presentation of Mary. The process may
have been more specific than we can now determine if we consider the
titles of Bale's lost plays dealing with such matters as the raising of
Lazarus, the Last Supper and the Washing of the Feet, the Passion, and
the Resurrection. Beyond this, however, Bale may have been seeking to
derive for his work in this genre some of the reputation of the existing
cycles. We have noted from time to time that his Protestant work not
only reacts against traditional Catholic material but also makes use of it
where Bale is impressed by it—as in his use of the antiphons in *God's
Promises*, and of quotations from the Vulgate. The same may be true of
his undertaking to recreate a cycle of scripture-based plays embodying
the new doctrines.

The question of the date of composition of a given play also could
have a political context. Although the designation of the actual dates of
composition of these three plays requires some caution, we should
observe that if they really were written after the more vociferous *Three
Laws* and *King Johan*, their more temperate tone may have been politically motivated. We can but suggest that, as the political climate grew
hotter after the events described in relation to *King Johan*, Bale may have
found it expedient to follow a more elevated and less provoking style.
Possibly the emphasis upon the likelihood of persecution for the enlightened Christian which is found in *Temptation* may also have been timely, as
Bale came to see that Henry's Protestantism was an uncertain and dangerous creation which needed to be controlled and directed:

> To persecucyon lete us prepare us than,
> For that wyll folowe in them that seke the truth. (ll. 19–20)

Even if there was a perceived need for caution, the plays had to embody
some essential Protestant features such as the vilification of the pope and
the Catholic hierarchy. Perhaps Bale felt he was on safer ground politically in suggesting in *The Temptation* that the pope was Satan's friend (l.
337), and in having Satan liken the scribes and the Pharisees to false
priests, bishops, and other servants (ll. 333–34). In the deepening crisis
for the Protestant interest in 1538 and 1539, especially with the promulgation of the Six Articles in May 1539, it might have come to seem
prudent to avoid writing about politically sensitive aspects of religious

controversy. In the same way the identification of superstition (treated in broad terms), of the possible exploitation of the poor, and of the misuse of military violence in respect of the three types of characters in *John Baptist's Preaching* may also have seemed safe subjects. It is always worth remembering that our knowledge of what has come to be seen as inevitable afterward would not prevent Bale and those who thought like him from hoping that it would not be so. The expectation of influencing events and altering consequences must have been alive.[5]

From a more specifically religious point of view, the plays embody certain important ideas and present them in similar ways. The perception of the harsh conflict between the inherent sinfulness of human beings and the inexorable justice of God is a significant trait. Protestantism is a religion based upon the upholding of God's law, and one which involves also the preaching of repentance. Hence the emergence of the Baptist as a powerful dramatic voice. It is a hard religion, but the functioning of divine grace within it is deeply consoling.

The faith presented here is also one intimately concerned with the Word as a means of exploring truth and motivation. The business of these plays is often a disputation, and the dynamic is toward the emergence of a purer truth. In the case of the arguments between Christ and Satan, the confrontation is deeply dramatic since the audience reaction is being controlled so that they see things differently from the characters. Traditions of characterization add much to the differentiation of language. This is accompanied by a process by which truth is tested; the plays are embodying the words of the Prolocutor in *The Temptation*:

The lyfe of Man is a profe or harde temptacyon. (l. 406)

There is for Bale an intimate link between proof and temptation by way of testing.

In *John Baptist's Preaching* the development of the play is concerned with the establishment of John's true role. There is a subtle interrelationship between his reluctance to baptize Christ on the grounds of his own unworthiness and Christ's exemplary submission to the law. The persuasion of John by Christ is critical to the developing awareness of true obedience:

If I by the lawe in yewth was circumcysed,
Why shuld I dysdayne thys tyme to be baptysed? (ll. 403–4)

Alongside such dramatic activity goes Bale's preoccupation with "declaration" by which he means revelation. In dramatic terms this shows itself in his emphasis upon dramatic signs. These are usually derived from biblical images, but not entirely so. The structure of *God's Promises* is arranged so that the role of each of the human figures could be marked with a sign, such as the rainbow used to show to Noah God's covenant with mankind. As it happens this particular sign does appear in the mystery cycles (as in the Chester *Noah*), and Bale thus follows the precedent. In other cases he invents business as in the intriguing stage direction in *God's Promises*:

> Here the Lord, extending his hand, touches John's lips with his fingers,
> and gives to him a tongue of gold. (l. 879, my translation)

It may be that Bale meant that God should actually give John a tongue of gold in the form of a stage property, as Blatt suggests (91); but however it was managed onstage, there is no doubting the importance of the symbolism. There is also no doubting that this is how Bale's dramatic imagination was tending in his concept of the action of this play.

We do not now know whether Bale sought publication for the lost biblical plays, but we can say that in choosing these three for printing he was addressing the key Protestant themes of prophecy, promise, repentance, and redemption in such a way that he could approach them through dramatic material relating to the law, temptation, and persecution. In order to achieve these he adapted or invented three different dramatic styles in a skillful manner.

Chapter Seven

Staging

To separate information about staging from discussion of the rest of Bale's dramatic achievement is clearly an artificial process, even though it may be convenient for quick reference. It has been made plain that the idea of putting what might seem to us somewhat intractable theological or political material on stage has many intimate connections with the way Bale thinks about his material and the problem or pleasure of how to communicate it effectively. It is sometimes difficult to decide whether the polemicist or the dramatist is supreme in his imagination. In many places in this study it has been possible to point to aspects which are effective on stage and which show skill in manifesting them. In principle, therefore, it is ill-advised to view staging as a separate item, and the value of this chapter should lie in how it shows that staging techniques enhance or realize the theatrical imagination which is also working with plot, characterization, and language, as already described.

A further justification for this chapter lies in the nature of drama itself. It is a sustainable view that no play exists in a purely textual form: Performance, whether directly influenced by the dramatist or not, is needed to bring out the theatrical qualities of the text. The paradox then arises that there is no such thing as a definitive performance; every performance has its own dynamic, which is partly a matter of how the audience influences what happens on stage. To make an extreme supposition, if the audience to *King Johan* did include King Henry (unlikely, but conceivable), the atmosphere would be quite different from that of an audience that included only Cranmer and/or Cromwell; and we can think of many other politically sensitive audiences. This is further compounded by the limitations of our ability to recall or reconstruct what did happen in any sixteenth-century performance, although we do at least know that there was a rich theatrical culture. Bale no doubt was aware of this culture and contributed to its development.

The culture may have been furthered by the state of the acting profession in the 1530s. There were certainly professional entertainers—people who derived their livings from being paid for such work, especially musicians. John Heywood is a case in point, in that he was paid at court when, as a boy and and a young man, he was a singer. Later he wrote and produced plays at court and was again paid for some of what he did, but he became a gentleman with property and a measure of prosperity and independence, partly due to royal gifts which may also be seen as a form of remuneration. Perhaps more important in his case, and bearing upon this argument, is the fact that he seems to have been continuously and extensively involved in entertainment as singer, performer, writer and producer over many years (from 1521 to 1558), although the degree and extent of his involvement must have varied according to court favor and the changes of political climate.[1]

Although Bale did apparently receive Cromwell's favor for some years, being directly involved in production, writing, and perhaps acting, the evidence that he had the same kind of lifelong commitment as Heywood is not strong. It looks as though after the period of Cromwell's support he had other priorities. Though he was interested in rewriting, editing, and publishing plays, he was not apparently interested in writing new ones, even though he did occasionally actively consider performances again.

Place

The texts yield limited information about the nature of the acting spaces required for the plays, although it is possible to deduce from them a sense of the metaphorical function of place they contain. There is little evidence of specific locations, of subdivisions of the acting area, or of structures on the stage. Even though the episodes in *God's Promises* each contain a dialogue between God and a human, there is no indication that God was placed at an upper level, though of course He could have been. Most of the action of *John Baptist's Preaching* is assumed to take place near the River Jordan, the scriptural location for the baptism of Christ. At the critical moment of baptism, there is no hint of the river in dialogue or stage direction: instead Bale's preoccupation is revealed in a specific movement:

> Here Jesus raises John and submits to him in baptism.
> (l. 421; my translation)

In *The Temptation*, Satan takes Christ to the traditional locations, two of which, the pinnacle of the temple and the mountain, are apparently elevated. In the case of the former, Christ refers to "gresynges" (steps; l. 203) by which he chooses to descend. In the French tradition such structures were large and elevated, but the scope of Bale's plays is much smaller and hardly implies the kind of civic expenditure available for the *Mystères*. No doubt a great deal could be achieved by very simple means. *The Temptation* is remarkable in that the movement from place to place is actually a required part of the action; there is very little that is similar elsewhere.

Such is the treatment of space in Bale's plays that often there is no specific location in which the action occurs. The management of the Pope, Usurped Power, in *King Johan* illustrates this clearly. The shift to Rome, or to some other place where the Pope could realistically be expected to be, is done silently and without foreshadowing. Suddenly, in the conversation it becomes apparent that Sedition and Dissimulation are in the presence of the Pope, who is not at this point dressed in papal robes (l. 832). There is little doubt that this surprise might be theatrically effective, and, further, it is appropriate to the allegorical dynamic we have identified in this play whereby characters are seen on multiple levels simultaneously. The location is thus more effective because it is in some sense imprecise and ambivalent. We might argue that this is an effective use of location from a dramatist who did not usually trouble very much about the verisimilitude of place, to the extent that very little is designated elsewhere in his work. In *Three Laws* the allegorical concept is simpler, and it is effectively presented on a stage which is entirely devoid of any sense of location; nor are there any areas of the stage which are used in specific ways.

For the biblical plays, as we have seen, the casting requirements seem to be for four parts, or indeed fewer. That two of the plays are marked for doubling raises further considerations of space. That the number of players is certainly limited to five in *Three Laws*, and probably to five in *King Johan*, suggests that Bale was working with a small company, and that therefore the stage would not be a large one. Nor perhaps could the onstage spectacle be dependent upon populous scenes. There is also the intriguing possibility that scribe A, most likely preparing the A text for performance, was trying to reduce the number of actors to four, though inconsistency in the directions for changes of role shows that he could not quite manage to do so. At no time in his part of the text are there more than four actors onstage, though a workable doubling scheme also has to be concerned with the amount of time available for changes of costume.[2]

Action

Limitations on stage space and on the number of players do not, however, prevent Bale from attempting remarkably effective and sometimes complex actions on the stage. These are related to the two different types of dramatization we have noted: the flexible, versatile, and often comic activities in *Three Laws* and especially in *King Johan* on the one hand, and the elevated effects of the biblical plays on the other. The derivation of *King Johan* from specifically historical sources gave a lead for certain episodes such as the excommunication and the poisoning, although even in the use of such material Bale's handling was highly selective and was directed towards the allegorical effects he had in mind. These would include, in comic vein, the satire on the papacy in the excommunication by means of the ritual involved. In this case the tone of the acting is perhaps not ridiculous so much as sinister. For the poisoning sequence, however, the stage manner is more complex. Primarily Johan is to be seen as dignified and perhaps tragic, though Bale does not use this word, while the poisoning is carried out by Dissimulation, a stage persona whom Bale has previously established as farcical, and who is now embodied in Simon of Swineshead. There is plenty of comic business to be found in the preparation of the draught; in Sedition's reassurance of Dissimulation that intercession of the saints and masses said in his honor will ease his way; in Dissimulation's absolution in advance by Sedition; in Sedition's comic song, "Wassayle, wassayle, out of the mylke payle" (ll. 2086–91); in the dividing of the draught; in Dissimulation's death agony; and in Dissimulation's final claim that, once sanctified, he will "do myracles in a whyle." It should be noted that some of this farcical material is played while Johan, accompanied by England, is on stage, so that the two effects are observable simultaneously. In this passage of the play there are no stage directions about the action. The only two stage directions are the exits for Sedition and England (ll. 2137 and 2192); the business and the contrasting tones are embedded in the dialogue.

Other remarkable stage actions include the long sequence of the "bringing in" of Sedition, discussed in chapter 5, where the effect is again farcical and where there is a notable sequence of physical actions and exploitation of offstage space in contrast to what is onstage. There is also the confession of Nobility, in which the words bring out the anti-Protestant nature of absolution, as well as Nobility's true duty to his king, while Sedition assumes the apparently impressive role of confessor. In these and other respects the action is likely to be dominated by Sedition carrying out the role of the Vice. Comic routines are inherent in this role, though it may not always be easy to say exactly how an actor would have managed them. The convention of this role, however, certainly came to be associated with rapid movement, skipping about, and antics which in general suggest tumbling and even acrobatics. How far Bale himself—if by any chance he took the role of the Vice—might have been able to do such things must remain engagingly speculative. However, there are plenty of ways, such as through soliloquies and asides, by which the Vice could invite the audience to perceive the comic role being enacted ("Is not thys a sport?" *King Johan*, l. 1682). The purpose was often to suggest a kind of ironic detachment from what the Vice was up to at the level of the plot; in short, Bale uses a metatheatrical presence which undoubtedly adds to the irony of the piece.

Both Sedition and Infidelity are involved in such gambols. The action of the two plays, *King Johan* and *Three Laws*, would depend in part upon the stage skill with which these parts were enacted. For example, when Infidelity is setting up his conspiracy in act 2 of *Three Laws*, he summons his two companions who are offstage:

> I conjure yow both here,
> And charge ye to apere,
>   Lyke two knaves as ye be! (ll. 386–88)

Sodomismus shouts from offstage, and Infidelity adds another piece of conjuring, using a magical word to summon spirits:

> By Tetragrammaton
> I charge ye, apere anon
>   And come out of the darke. (ll. 392–94)

Whereupon a stage direction marks their entry, and Sodomismus appears singing a snatch of song, while Idololatria is wheezing and coughing.

Another feature of the vice's part is the opportunity to show off in "performing" a list. To a reader, a list of the various relics may seem rather quaint, but it is surely a performer's dream. In his revision Bale took the trouble to add to the original list enumerated by Sedition. Even though some of the items on the list can be traced to the atmosphere of controversy at the time, the gain is also beneficial to the performer. Did he really pull them one by one out of his pocket or his pack, like Chaucer's Pardoner? What business did he use to indicate the bad smells?

> Here ys fyrst a bone of the blyssyd Trinity,
> A dram of the tord of swete [sweet?] Seynt Barnabe . . .
> A maggott of Moyses, with a fart of Saynt Fandigo.

In its enlarged form the passage is 16 lines long and includes many
rhythmic variations (ll. 1215–30). It may be a bit crude, but there is no
doubting its stage potential.

The discussion of the biblical plays in chapter 6 showed that their
dramatic style is different in general from that of the other two plays.
This is manifested in the action onstage. The absence of comic effects,
including the Vice as the center of them, and the emphasis upon symbolic actions to mark critical moments in the biblical narratives and situations give these plays a special stage manner. This is partly a structural
matter, as we have seen, but we also note that the idea of the sign is central to the activities upon stage. Thus much is made of the symbols of
God's promises, of the golden tongue given to Joannes Baptista, and of
the significant kneeling of Christ at the baptism.

Closely associated with this emphasis upon signs are the differing
natures of the other types of action. One type is the need to enact certain
parts of the scriptural narratives, as in the presentation of the three
temptations and the baptizing of Christ. These actions endorse the
authority of the plays, and since they involve events also found in the
traditional cycles but have a different ethos, they challenge the interpretation of these events by their very occurrence. In a sense Bale has to
register them in action in order to authenticate his doctrinal position,
even though he departs markedly from the exegetical traditions which
had grown up around them. There is also an underlying interest in the
reasons why Bale chooses to omit some actions or events.

In the biblical plays the dialogue, considered as an exchange of views,
or indeed as a testing of opposing points, is a marked feature. To some
extent the prominence given to certain exchanges is essential to the
plays. The exchanges are the action of the plays, which should not be
seen as undramatic, even though the passages of dispute do not show
much physical action. This is especially so in *John Baptist's Preaching*
where there is both preaching and argument between John and the
other characters. In *Temptation* the tense verbal exchanges are accompanied by movement to the three scriptural places for tempting. But the
interest lies equally strongly upon the exchanges between Christ and
Satan, especially as Bale is able to give to many of Satan's speeches a dramatic irony which plays around him whether he is speaking the truth or
not, or whether or not he speaks more truly than he is aware.

There are requirements for music in all five extant plays. In the biblical plays the range is dramatically narrower. In *John Baptist's Preaching*
and in *The Temptation*, songs appear only once; in each at a moment of

triumph. John sings a Gloria after the baptism, and two angels sing an unspecified "sweet song" after Christ has triumphed over Satan. We have noted that the Advent antiphons are systematically interwoven into each of the seven acts of *God's Promises*, again at climactic moments. The presence of all these items argues the importance of music in Bale's concept of drama in these plays, and it also suggests that he had access to singers who could perform adequately. No doubt his own experience as a Carmelite helped.

In *Three Laws* there are seven places where music is required (leaving aside the macaronic and Protestantized Benedictus at the end of the printed text, a segment that may not have been part of the performance); in *King Johan* there are eight. In both cases the Vice is the principal singer, though he does take part in songs with other characters in some items. His association with the music has two functions. One is an identifying process whereby he sings on entry, suggesting his own brand of irreverent humor and usually changing the preceding atmosphere on stage. Thus Infidelity comes in with a version of a street cry, in which he offers brooms in exchange for boots, shoes, buskins, and "powcheryngs" (ll. 176–80). He also sings to express solidarity or success with his associates (l. 698 s.d.). This process of identification may be linked to popular song. The information is somewhat sketchy, perhaps because Bale did not think it necessary to specify what was to be sung in places (as at ll. 1219 s.d.), but Infidelity does ask for "a myry songe" (l. 696) and also does a bit of song and dance in:

And make frowlyke chere, with hey how, fryska jolye. (l. 1754)

Sedition reintroduces himself late in the play with a snatch of song:

Pepe I see ye! I am glad I have spyed ye! (l. 2457)

The manuscript gives a stave of music which has not been positively matched with any surviving piece but is thought to be a popular song.

Another function of music in Bale's plays is to ridicule the liturgy. This is done briefly by Infidelity with his bawdy tale about "stones" (*Lapides preciosi*, ll. 814–19) in the reported duet between the monk and the nun. Infidelity sings both parts, perhaps moving about the stage to animate the two different voices in a kind of dialogue, perhaps singing falsetto for the nun and bass for the monk. Bale elsewhere composes a liturgical parody:

Da quaesumus ut sicut eorum sudoribus vivimus ita eorum uxoribus, filiabus et domicellus perpetuo frui mereamur.[3]

In contrast, there is one serious incorporation of religious music in this play, as the Laws celebrate their recovery with Psalm 113, "or some similar song" (l. 1913 s.d.). This is preceded by a paraphrase of part of the *Nunc dimittis* ("Now leavest thy servauntes in thy perpetual peace; ll. 1902–10), though apparently this is not sung.

The ridicule of the liturgy is more extensive in *King Johan*. It is used as part of the introduction of characters as well: for Dissimulation (ll. 636–50) and for Usurped Power and Private Wealth in the transit to Rome discussed above (ll. 764–65). The attack is more guarded over Johan's submission, for he sings a *Confiteor* to which Sedition responds as Stephen Langton. This is intriguing because Sedition's part contains no ridicule, though this is not to say that he might not perform apparently serious words in a derogatory manner. Certainly Bale's purpose in using liturgy at this point seems to be to present the outrageous nature of Johan's enforced submission. The attitude of the audience to this liturgical quotation here might also contribute something to the tone of the performance.

Costumes and Properties

The nature and use of costumes and properties in Bale's plays are intimately related to the varying dramatic modes we have been discussing. Though he had no systematic approach to recording or specifying costumes and properties, many details about them can be deduced from the dialogue and the stage directions. In the catalog made by the present author there are nearly 100 references, some of which are multiple.[4] Such a large amount of information makes it clear that although Bale may have left the locations of his plays rather uncertain, he had many specific ideas about what his characters should look like and how they should employ properties. These ideas are so well developed that his use of these visual items is tantamount to an iconography, and one which is aimed at the symbolic and satirical objectives which are an integral part of the argument he offers. Since many details of costumes and properties have already appeared in the analysis of the plays, the details adduced here will be selective.

In the biblical plays Bale was no doubt able to rely upon costumes traditional in the cycles. His main concern was to turn them into a comment upon the craftiness and corruption of the Catholic clergy. In order to do this he used religious and legal robes; perhaps the former were in plentiful supply as the Dissolution of the Monasteries in 1536 made many garments superfluous to their former owners. It is true too that with the religious changes now occurring, people would naturally be more sensitive about the garments of the old religion, whether they were sympathetic to the changes or not. Ecclesiatical costumes such as those worn by Usurped Power, Private Wealth, and Dissimulation would have a strong contemporary value, which Bale wanted to be negative. The idea of the significance of such costumes in real life is elaborated by Sedition in a long speech in which he describes the extent of his many disguises. He obviously cannot wear all these at the same time, but in describing them there is presumably an opportunity for mime and gesture. The passage begins:

Sumtyme I can be   a monke in a long syd cowle;
Sumtyme I can be   a none and loke lyke an owle;
Sumtyme a channon   in a syrples fayer and whyght . . . (see ll. 195–210)

By the end of the passage he envisages himself as a pope.

Dissimulation specifically draws attention in speech, and with accompanying vain gestures no doubt, to the assortment of monastic habits he is manifestly wearing:

Nay, *dowst thow not se   how I in my colours jette?*
This is for Bernard,   and this is for Benet,
This is for Gylbard,   and this is for Jhenet;
For Frauncys this is,   and this is for Domynyke,
For Awsten and Elen,   and this for Seynt Partryk. (ll. 726–29; my italics)

Infidelity's description of a similar mixture in the clothing of Sodomismus in *Three Laws* brings the dramatic impact close to the identity of a fool:

The fellawe is wele decked,
Dysgysed and wele necked,
Both knavebalde and pypecked,
He lacketh nothynge but bels. (ll. 622–25)

Another effect is achieved by Infidelity's interpretation of the significance of Ambitio's miter. He suggests that there are "tropes and types"

expressed in it, and to demonstrate his meaning, he has Ambitio bend
forward so that the top of the miter becomes a gaping mouth:

> If thu stoope downewarde, loo, se how the wolfe doth gape. (l. 1185)

He adds that by means of the three crowns of a papal tiara he will conceal Ambitio's wolvishness.

Alongside this satirical and comic identification of character by costume comes the device of changing appearances. Satan in *Temptation*,
having said that he must put on a "godly pretence . . . semynge relygyouse," (ll. 74–75) presumably changes his costume. The likelihood is
that if he does change onstage—and there is no apparent time for him to
go off—he does it by having a second costume underneath.[5] There is no
doubt that changing costume onstage can be a powerful theatrical event,
whether putting on or taking off! This would apply in the treatment of
Evangelium in *Three Laws*, where his garments are removed and dirtier
ones put on him as the Vices torment him in preparation for execution
(l. 1726 s.d.). For Sedition, Usurped Power, Private Wealth, and Treason
("a pryste," l. 1810) in *King Johan*, there is the added dimension that a
change of costume carries forward an aspect of meaning, as the historical
characters are to be seen as manifesting the underlying and more perma-
nent evil abstractions. In these cases we must suppose that some link
between the abstract character and the historical one could be manifest
to the audience visually; there would be no point in the identification if
Sedition disappeared completely into the role of Stephen Langton. Thus
the costume change is intimately linked to the dynamic of performance.
At Nobility's request, Sedition puts on a stole to hear confession, an
action which has ritual concomitants if done correctly.

The colophon of *Three Laws* sheds some light on Bale's thinking
about costume. As he obviously wanted to be specific about the three
pairs of Vices, "the frutes of Infidelyte," he prescribes costumes for each
of them, including Idolatria as a witch and Sodomismus as a monk of
all sects. At the end of the list he says, "The rest of the partes are easye
ynough to conjecture" (G1ᵛ). This must mean that the other characters
follow conventional clothing, or their costumes may be deduced from
the text itself. Interestingly, this leaves us uncertain about what might be
the conventional costume for the vice.

Such a procedure about conventional costuming would no doubt suit
angels well enough, and it might also be appropriate for historical characters such as Pharisaeus and Sadducaeus, and for John the Baptist, for

whom there would be plenty of dramatic or iconological precedents. It would also apply neatly to typed characters such as Civil Order, Nobility and Clergy in *King Johan*. There would be some point in differentiating Clergy's costume from that of Dissimulation. Even Widow England wears clothes which make her role apparent. Moreover, Johan comments that she is "chaungyd thus," which she makes clear refers to the poor state of her clothing brought about by the clergy who have impoverished her (ll. 42–59). Sometimes characters who undergo a change of fortune are also made to change their appearance as with the blindness of Commonalty (*King Johan*, ll. 1550–51), and the leprosy, blindness, and lameness imposed upon Law of Nature and Law of Moses (*Three Laws*, ll. 758 and 1264).

Many of the hand properties specified in the text or the stage directions are commonplace items obtainable from a domestic source or a props box. They require little comment, except that they show that some part of Bale's dramaturgy was rooted in practical details of a realistic nature, and that he conceived of action on stage as needing these simple supports. Typical items are the book and various documents, such as a letter; but the obligation might also be pretentiously elaborate, such as the crown, the potion, the food brought by the angels, and Infidelity's brooms.

There are properties, however, which have much more meaning attached, and this concerns the continuing ridicule of the Catholic ritual and also positive symbolism. Both Sedition's list of relics, which include a bone, a feather, a tooth, a harp string, milk, a scab, a nail of Adam's toe, a lachet, a rib, and a knucklebone (*King Johan*, ll. 1215–30), and the gear which Infidelity offers to Sodomismus and Idololatria, including beads, rings, pins, a staff, and a scrip (*Three Laws*, ll. 659–70), suggest the superficiality of Catholic preoccupation, not to mention its merchandizing. No doubt there would be great antics involved in showing off these objects. In other cases, the paraphernalia of ritual would need to be used to show a sinister threat. Here the bell, book, and candle, or the chains, would be employed.

There are also symbolic items. In the first Act of *Three Laws*, God shows the heart to Nature, gives tables (tablets of stone) to Moses, and gives a New Testament to Christ. It is not very clear how these symbols would be managed, but they need to be visible because they are referred to again in act 5 where their significance is reaffirmed. Equally complex is the way Infidelity is overwhelmed in the same act. As the stage directions here are in Latin, there may be some doubt about whether this part of the play was ever actually performed; but if it were, the first requirement would be that Vindicta Dei throw water on Infidelity, the second that he strike him with a sword, and the third that he drive him out with fire. That these items had a symbolic importance is borne out by the fact that each can be traced to a biblical source (Genesis 6:17; Leviticus 26:26; Psalms 96:3). Similarly the descent of the dove in *Temptation* is scriptural, but in this case there are precedents for managing such an effect, as in the stage device for representing the dove's return in the Chester play of *Noah* (play 3, l. 260).

Chapter Eight

John Bale and Sixteenth-Century Literature

The account of John Bale's work presented in this book should make plain that although he has had a somewhat questionable reputation for many years, his literary interests were very wide indeed. Perhaps it is time to take a more balanced look at what he achieved in his own lifetime, as well as his later impact. This would include a significant reappraisal of the "bilious" epithet ascribed to Bale by Thomas Fuller[1], and a closer look at his prose and verse styles. He lived in a period of acute change, and he touched and reflected contemporary events in many ways. A full estimate of his reaction to his own time and culture and to his influence upon what followed would be enough for a volume in itself. Here we shall concentrate on the two major divisions treated in the present volume—his nondramatic work and his plays—but such a division should not obscure the fact that most of his work is integrated into his (sometimes acrimonious) vision of the Christian's life and responsibilities. This includes both his attempt to rewrite history, and his development of several literary and dramatic forms to such an end. It is clear that even after his conversion there was some evolution in his central beliefs, but it is still to be noted that his work as a whole has a coherent rationale and purpose.

Nondramatic Works

The two main thrusts in Bale's nondramatic works were his enormous application to the gathering of information about earlier writers (mostly but not entirely English) and his rewriting of history with a Protestant intent. Both were influential. The catalogs he assembled remain an invaluable resource for scholars wanting to investigate the history of literature, not least because Bale's literary criteria were pre-Renaissance, pre-Shakespearean, pre-Romantic, and pre-modern. Because of this stance, unconscious of the modern literary canon, he shows us a world and a culture which would otherwise be more dimly apprehended. This is especially true of the information about Carmelite writers, an ironic survival in his Protestant world, as well as that about early Wycliffite and Protestant writers. In this part of his work as a biographer and cata- loger, he worked in parallel with Conrad Gesner, according to an ancient tradition which, as far as we know, had not previously been applied to British writers. He was followed most notably by Flacius, who acknowl- edges Bale as an authority early, as in his *Catalogus* (Basel, 1562). In his *Historia Ecclesiastica* (Magdeburg, 1560-74), as John N. King points out, Flacius used Bale's apocalyptic historiography as developed in the *Image*.[2] A counterblast from a Catholic viewpoint was compiled by John Pitts in his *Relationum Historicarum de Rebus Anglicis* (Paris, 1619). He is quick to attack Bale for his heresy, calumny, and ingratitude and for his criticism of the papacy (9). He reviews the history of religion in England from a Catholic viewpoint, and sharply attacks Wyclif and Bale's defense of him, quoting verbatim from Bale's eulogy in order to deny it. He claims that, in editing the work of John Leland, Bale deliberately obscured it. It is clear, however, that Pitts closely follows the method and layout of Bale's *Catalogus*; to do this is, of course, a means of casting further oblo- quy upon it.

Although Bale's particular apocalyptic rendering of history was unac- ceptable to some, there is little doubt that the recurring image of eccle- siastical conflict on a cosmic scale became a central idea for many writers, including Spenser and Milton. It is important to note that this image was transmitted by the publication and reprinting of several of Bale's works. These include the *Image*, *Votaries*, and the *Acta Romanorum Pontificum* (originally part of the *Catalogus*, translated into English by John Studley as *The Pageant of Popes* and printed in 1574). Had he not been so assiduous in seeking the publication, which must have generat- ed knowledge of his work, Bale's achievement would have had less impact. In this respect he showed himself to be aware of the value of the development of printing in the dissemination of information and opin- ion. His continuing attention to illustration through woodcuts in many of his printed works is symptomatic. It should be noted, however, that he was of sufficient importance to some of his contemporaries for some of his work to be reprinted in the years immediately after his death, including *Three Laws* (1572) and *God's Promises* (1577).

Perhaps one of the most influential vehicles for the transmission of Bale's ideas and methods was John Foxe's *Acts and Monuments* (1563), a book to be found in many public places and in many households for gen- erations. We have seen how the two worked alongside one another for several years, and it is likely that Bale's meticulous approach to documentary information influenced Foxe. It certainly seems that Foxe used some of the same documents as Bale—for example, those pertaining to Anne Askew and John Oldcastle. Most impressive, from a modern point of view, is that Bale tended to use contemporary documents in his work; he explored libraries, cataloging and collecting, as the source of this direct method; Foxe followed him in this. In fact, Bale's historical method is not always scrupulously factual. Sometimes he edits documents to give a strong twist to depositions and interrogations—"paraphrastically," as he put it. We have seen that in *King Johan* he was inclined to ignore the reading of chronicles when it happened not to suit his purpose; like Satan in *Temptation*, he sometimes left out what he did not fancy because "It made not for me" (l. 242). In spite of this, he and Foxe did provide historical narratives which are often capable of being checked from the sources they adduced, and this is a valuable way of "making" history. The work of both men has thus proved a treasury for later critical historians of religion, politics and literature.

The link between Bale and Foxe is also strong in the interpretation of history. Foxe seems to have followed Bale's scheme of the chronology and structure of history, including the influence of Constantine and the degeneracy of the papacy, especially in the time of Wyclif, "the age of locusts." Although Foxe is rarely as outspoken as Bale in the denigration of his opponents, there is little doubt that he carried forward Bale's interpretation. Aspects of this interpretation, because of the popularity of *Acts and Monuments*, became central to Protestant culture in England and remained so for centuries. Most especially the two writers between them created a Protestant martyrology, and provided a means by which the new martyrs were celebrated and could, in some measure, speak for themselves. To differentiate between the two writers, it should also be said that Foxe's work as a historian has perhaps achieved a higher reputation than Bale's because he developed the presentation of documentary evidence even further. The extent of the influence of Bale's apocalyptic views on the accession of Elizabeth I may be judged by the use of the commentary in *Image* for marginal annotations in the Puritan Geneva Bible (1560).[3]

Probably Bale's shorter and more polemical works were less well known and less influential. As we have seen, many of them turn on particular political situations which proved ephemeral, and with the changing of circumstances the arguments may have become less intriguing. However, they do voice an intensity of feeling, and in spite of some intemperate language at times, they speak firmly and passionately of his beliefs, and those of many others. In a more remarkable way, perhaps, the *Vocation* presents a personal account of a difficult experience. It is not easy to tell whether this book became well known, though it certainly did draw a riposte. Its type, however, as an autobiographical narrative facing adversity but acknowledging divine support, may well have had imitators right through to the fictionalized *Robinson Crusoe*. One of its great strengths is that it is a narrative about a journey, anticipating *Pilgrim's Progress*. There is certainly a link between the urgency of this personal writing and the emphasis on documentary evidence noted above. In both cases the idea of the "witness" becomes more explicit.[4]

The Plays

Since Collier's rediscovery and publication of *King Johan* in 1838, Bale has figured in histories of literature and the drama, and in influential anthologies. There is thus no doubt that this one play has become one of the chief ways by which the drama of the sixteenth century has been perceived, located, and taught. The extensive development of knowledge of his other plays, and of the whole corpus of late medieval and Tudor drama in the past 25 years, has not really brought about significant change in the estimate of his relative importance. However, there may have been a shift of emphasis worth noting, not least because his reputation for vitriolic attacks has seriously obscured the positive quality of his work. He attracted most attention, to begin with, because *King Johan* could be read as a history play and perhaps as a tragedy, anticipating Shakespeare. It still seems to be true that Bale's desire to see patterns and structures in history may have influenced Shakespeare directly or, more likely, indirectly, but now there is very little that can be adduced to show that Shakespeare knew Bale's play (we assume it remained an unpublished manuscript), though he probably knew *Acts and Monuments*, which does deal with Johan's death in a somewhat similar vein. In any event, Shakespeare's own play took very different directions.

Two other extant plays show that Bale's concern with state policies and kingship may have had a broad reference. Though *King Johan* may not have been widely known, it is possible that the author of *Respublica*, which was addressed to Queen Mary, owes something to it, perhaps because he might have been aware of what was going on at government level. This play uses comic and satirical material, including the named Vice, Avarice, to satirize Protestant abuses, especially materialism and economic exploitation, which had allegedly preceded Mary's accession and had presumably been perpetrated by Somerset and North-umberland. The onstage devices, working through a group of villains led by Avarice and involving impersonation, wordplay, and trickery of many kinds, suggest a very skillful dramatist. (The attribution to Nicholas Udall, however, is still open to doubt.) The intention is to draw attention to abuses, but also to reveal Mary's potential as a means of redressing wrongs. The balance of the polemic in the play, however, suggests an attempt to pour oil on troubled waters rather than to inflame the politi-cal and religious divide; perhaps it was written at the beginning of the new reign in the hope of preventing an anticipated hardening of atti-tudes by means of stage ridicule.

There seems to be less likelihood that Sir David Lindsay knew Bale's play; his known visit to the English court occurred well before its pre-sumed writing. However his *Ane Satire of the Thrie Estaitis* shares some aspects of Bale's Protestant standpoint, especially his criticism of Church abuses. The methods he uses also involve intensive ridicule and a deep sense of outrage about clerical avarice, based upon practices such as mor-tuary gifts to parish priests, the worship of the saints, and the unchastity of the regular clergy. The business is enhanced by a versatile group of stage villains led by Flatterie, dressed as a friar. These show similar shifti-ness, word games and trickery, as well as the manipulation of names and aliases noted in Bale's work. Lindsay's position in controversy was a deli-cate one. He was a lifelong courtier, at times personally very close to the monarch, and it may well be that the first version of his play, noted at the Scottish court in 1540 but without a surviving text, was generated by a desire to see reforms without necessarily being disposed to embrace the Reformation comprehensively. In any case Lindsay was no doubt adept in treading warily, as the selection of ideas to be attacked becomes plain. It looks as though he was practicing a form of self-censorship. The play was revived in 1552 and 1553, the latter performance being at Edinburgh with the support of the Queen Regent. The differences between *King Johan* and these two plays are quite as important as the similarities. Nevertheless it looks as though Bale was one of the first to deal openly with a need to express the tensions of the Reformation in stage terms, and that others followed him in somewhat different contexts.

The modern study of interludes, a rather imprecise term which Bale himself employed along with other contemporaries, has led to some dif-ferences in the perception of his achievement. This study has shown that all Bale's plays have strong stage potential, and that, writing when he did, he was probably one of the most successful proponents of the inter-

lude. He certainly seems to have grasped some of the essential strengths
of this particular type of play. Moreover, the relatively early date suggests that, as his work was published and performed, it might have been
quite well known by 1550. The further development of the interlude
after that date is an important element in the development of the
Elizabethan theater; historians are now inclined to see continuity in
many aspects of the drama, from the interludes through to Shakespeare
and his contemporaries. Although it is likely that the interlude owed
much to such moralities as *Mankind* and *Wisdom*, the genre of the morality in the fifteenth century is rather shadowy. Before Bale we know of
only a few interludes, of which John Skelton's *Magnyfycence* is the most
likely to have influenced him, since it was written for the ambience of
the Court and printed about 1530.

The belated issuing of Skelton's play may well have been a contributory
factor in the publication of John Heywood's interludes in the years
1533–34. There are certainly a number of elements which suggest a possible debt to Skelton. It now seems likely that Heywood's publications
were actually contributing to the rapidly changing political and religious
debate over the king's divorce. If this is so, Heywood provides a possible
stimulus to Bale's intervention in these matters, under the influence of
Cromwell. It is even possible that Cromwell intervened to inhibit printing of Catholic material by William Rastell, Heywood's printer and
brother-in-law.[5]

Heywood's plays are very different from Bale's in many respects, but
it is at least tenable that between them they made the major contribution to the development of the interlude as a dramatic form in the
1530s. Heywood, a Catholic who cannily eschewed confrontation,
sought by laughter to attack both Catholic abuses and Protestant excesses, and he did this in an oblique way which attempted to avoid any risk
of dangerous accusation. In this way he circumspectly bears witness to
the fear of persecution we have noted in Bale. He structured his plays
around confrontation between speakers offering different views, and was
very careful about giving support or implying approval. Although his
plays are based upon abstract characterization and might therefore owe
something to the morality plays, they are different from most of Bale's
drama inasmuch as the majority of his characters are social types who
might conflict in real life but whose confrontation does not take place in
an allegorical structure.

Heywood's work preceded Bale's, as far as we can tell; Bale notes
some of Heywood's titles in the *Summarium* and and the *Catalogus* (*Love*,

Wether, and *Four PP*). His praise of Heywood's wit indicates that, although Bale did not apparently move in the court circles frequented by Heywood, he was aware of his work. Bale thought he did nothing to promote truth, being adverse to it (*Catalogus* II, 110). But again the fact of Heywood's publication in 1533 and 1534 is perhaps significant in generating awareness of it.

In length and scope, Heywood's plays are somewhat similar to Bale's, although there is no indication of doubling—quite the reverse, presumably because his plays were meant to be performed by boys at court. They are like Bale's in some theatrical aspects; they depend upon an intimate relationship with the audience, as, for example, when John John asks a member of the audience to hold his coat, and to scrape off the dirt while he is at it (*Johan Johan*, ll. 250–57). It is in Heywood's use of the vice, however, that he comes closest to Bale, or at least offers Bale an idea to develop. Merry Report is named the Vice on the title page of *Wether*, and Neither Loving nor Loved is called the Vice in a stage direction requiring outrageously ridiculous costuming and acting in *Love* (ll.1297).[6] As far as we know, these are the first occasions when the vice was named as a stage role in a play text. Heywood's two characters are up to all sorts of tricks. They are chiefly mischievous and troublesome to others, offering bawdy and and other verbal games, and showing remarkable physical dexterity at times. Working from their special positions, Merry Report, as the servant of Jupiter and controlling access to him, and Neither Loving nor Loved as the one character who, he claims, is not affected by love, they are able to manipulate the other characters and to mock them. Because Heywood is not in pursuit of a moral allegory, however, they do not have a strictly evil characterization, as their names make clear. Instead of using Heywood's humanist dialogue of carefully matched and contrasted colors, Bale went for the kind of polemical attack we have discussed, and for this purpose the stage effectiveness of the Vice, already developed by Heywood, was convenient. Once Bale got hold of this stage device, he extended it, and so of course did almost all the writers of interludes who followed him up until about 1580. Perhaps because of the centrality of the vice, who could be used to mock Catholic practices, the interlude became more and more a vehicle for religious controversy. Since, apart from the reign of Queen Mary, the government and therefore the control of licensing were in Protestant hands, the bulk of those interludes which have survived were Protestant in outlook. It is in these plays that some influence of Bale may be discerned.

Bale's Influence

It is not evident, of course, that there was anything like a "school" of
Bale. Indeed the difficulty is partly that because Bale incorporated main-
stream Protestant preoccupations, often to be derived directly by others
from Tyndale or perhaps Luther, it is not always possible to attribute
influence to him. Moreover, as *King Johan* was presumably not printed, it
is possible that there is influence from other interludes later than 1538
before Bale made the additions which included, it will be remembered,
some enlargements of the part of Sedition, who, though not so named,
carries out the function of the Vice. What we can see is that a number of
dramatists from midcentury onward used the interlude, with its characteristic stage vitality, but arranged for a small number of actors with a
linear and alternating structure designed to allow the groups of vices and
virtues to be played in turn by the same few actors.[7] These plays pursued
Protestant aims in a didactic mode.

Here we shall consider briefly four plays in this genre, each of which
shows signs of being written in ways similar to Bale's plays. Richard
Wever's *Lusty Juventus*, composed about 1550 and printed by 1553, and
Lewis Wager's *Life and Repentance of Mary Magdalene*, written before 1553
and printed in 1566, each owe something to other, older genres. *Lusty
Juventus* is a play about youth which gives a picture of the dangers
attending on the young. This theme had appeared in several Catholic
plays, but from now on it was to be much addressed in the Protestant
interludes, attracted no doubt by the Prodigal Son motif from scripture.
The question of education became very topical. Hypocrisy, the Vice, is
the son of the Devil, and in a scene with him he supports a desire to go
back to the ways of Catholicism. He lists many devices he has used to try
to bring this about, a list which seems to echo many of Bale's preoccupations with the details of Catholic ritual and practice. It begins:

> As holy [Cardinalls, holy Popes,]
> Holy vest[iments, holy copes,]
> Holy armettes and Friers,
> Holy priestes, holy bisshopes.[8]

He adopts the alias Friendship (ll. 488–89) and indulges in dicing in
order to entrap the hero. As the action turns back to virtue, a character
called God's Promises comes on to reveal the truth (l. 1050).

Lewis Wager's play draws perhaps from the genre of the saint play.
We have noted that Bale seemed interested in this, in his construction of

King Johan as a virtuous leader who was martyred. Mary Magdalene offered the special attraction to Protestants of being scriptural, even though her role had traditionally been an accretion of two women in the Bible who were not necessarily the same person. Lewis Wager, like Bale, was a friar who had turned Protestant, and it is likely that he brought with him some aspects of his former belief. However, his position is more influenced by Calvin than Bale's was. His Vice is Infidelity, who represents Catholic evils; he admits to being the source of all iniquities. The Vice works much as he did in Bale. He leads a group of other vices and uses different disguises. At one point he admits to having a cap and gown (l. 404), and later a Pharisee's gown (l. 1522).[9] He refers to himself as having the name Moysaicall Justice in Jewry (l. 21). Although this is not further developed, it seems reminiscent of the way Sedition is revealed in another role. Near the end of the play he adopts the alias Legal Justification (l. 1899), a character who is contrasted with the virtuous Justification, and who, in the Protestant mode of the play, explains that Faith leads to Justification. The emphasis upon Law, not dissimilar to Bale's, leads to the doctrine that Christ came to bring Love, and so to fulfill it. Love is thus seen as a fruit of forgiveness and not as something which is deserved (ll. 2004–5). While the doctrinal position and emphasis are thus not exactly the same as Bale's, it seems very likely that the thinking of Lewis Wager was quite similar. A further hint lies in the reference to "God's promission," which seems to sum up much of Bale's play:

> This faith is founded on God's promission,
> And most clerely to the mynde of man revealed,
> So that of God's will he hath an intuition,
> Which by the holy Ghost to his heart is sealed. (ll. 1382–85)

At the beginning of Elizabeth's reign, somewhat later than these two plays, the anonymous *New Custom* (1564–71), and William Wager's *Enough Is as Good as a Feast* (?1570) show further adaptations of doctrines like Bale's in interludes which seem to echo his dramatic technique.[10] The former has two pairs of clergy, Perverse Doctrine and Hypocrisy versus New Custom and Light of the Gospel, and is much concerned with the fear of Catholic restoration. There is an attack upon Catholic items including "Crosses, bells, candells, oyle, bran, salt, spettle and incence."[11]

William Wager may have been the son of Lewis Wager. He became a Protestant clergyman of distinction, working in several London parishes. *Enough is as Good as a Feast* has the significant variation of having two heroes, Heavenly Man and Worldly Man. The former has the consolation of God's promises (l. 143) while the latter seems to extend the fate of the sinner toward tragedy, since much of the business of the play is to show his decline into sin, ending with a death scene in the presence of the named Vice, Covetous, and Ignorance. Worldly Man is a stark example of the fate of the unrepentant sinner, the underlying principle being the Doctrine of the Elect. The action of the play is enhanced by his refusal, even to the last, to think about anything but the fraudulent disposal of his wealth. The role of Covetous contains many conventional characteristics of the vice. He has a song about himself (l. 281); he fights with a dagger (l. 440); he changes his and others' names (l. 473); he laughs and weeps excessively (l. 511 and ll. 700–710); he has a long, nonsense soliloquy beginning "A Blackheath field where great Golias was slain," (ll. 305–52); he boasts of his superiority ("I govern all," l. 917); and in general he manipulates the conspiracy. He is supported by a spectacular appearance by Satan, who comes on roaring, and who gloats over the sins of Worldly Man and his death without grace, declaring to his soul that he has earned a ride off to hell on the Devil's back:

> Come on mine own boy, go thou with me,
> Thou hast served me duly and hatest me never;
> Therefore now for thy pains rewarded shalt thou be
> In everlasting fire that burneth forever.
> *Bear him out upon his back.* (ll. 1468–71)

This is a highly disciplined play in an intellectual mode, and it manages a cast of 18 characters played by seven actors very dextrously. It looks as though William Wager was an experienced dramatist well able to make his theological point by stage devices, and that he wrote in the expectation of performance.

These four interludes may be taken as an indication that Bale's plays, in terms of his religious stance as well as his dramatic methods, may well have been influential in his own lifetime and in the years immediately after his death. It appears that the interlude was well suited to being a vehicle for religious propaganda, and there is little doubt that, whether these dramatists knew his work or not, he is likely to have been influential in generating this particular dramatic mode and some of its most notable ingredients.

We have noted that *King Johan* has what amounts to a tragic effect in the death of the hero. It would probably not be wise to claim a significant rediscovery of tragedy for the stage until the second half of the century. Nevertheless, the seriousness of moral dilemmas and their striking emotional effect, together with an awareness of divine wrath, do become apparent in some midcentury interludes.[12] We may note a developing consciousness of the dramatic form in two aspects. The first is the use of the word "tragedy" itself, which we have remarked in Bale's text of *Three Laws* (l. 1425), as well as on the title page of *God's Promises*. Lewis Wager has Pride say:

> In our tragedie we may not use our owne names. (l. 365)

The second aspect is that the Protestant necessity for repentance and judgment, supported perhaps by the Doctrine of the Elect, leads to the portrayal of characters like Worldly Man (and also Moros in William Wager's *The Longer Thou Livest the More Fool Thou Art*), who are unredeemed, and unredeemable without repentance. The need to show by terrible example becomes an ingredient for tragedy that was later much exploited by Elizabethan tragedians.

Also interesting in this context is Bale's early use of the word "Comedie" in his titles, a characteristic followed by many other sixteenth-century playwrights: *Enough* follows this convention, and there are many others such as *Longer* and Thomas Lipton's *All for Money*. Even more common in titles is the word "interlude," which goes back to the generation before Bale, at least as far back as *Youth*, *Hickscorner*, Skelton's *Magnyfycence*, and Medwall's *Nature*, which were all printed by about 1530. Although it is difficult to establish exactly what the dramatists or their printers actually meant by such ascriptions—indeed there will hardly be a precise meaning for each—the use of all three terms, subscribed to by Bale, is an indication of the rich, varied, and notably self-conscious development of the art of drama in the sixteenth century—the art of which Bale made a comprehensive appraisal and to which he made such a signal contribution.

Notes and References

Chapter One

1. The chief bibliographical and biographical works on John Bale are by Thora Balslev Blatt, William T. Davies, Leslie P. Fairfield (1976), Jesse W. Harris, Ritchie D. Kendall, John N. King, and Honor C. McCusker. These will be found in the Selected Bibliography.

2. Although Bale's membership in Jesus College has been questioned, the evidence in favor of it is circumstantial in John Sherman's manuscript, *Aborigines Jesuani*, in the College archives. Bale also speaks of Geoffrey Downes, a fellow of the College, as his father in theology (*Catalogus*, 632).

3. L. P. Fairfield, "*The Vocacyon of Johan Bale* and Early English Autobiography," *Renaissance Quarterly* 24 (1971): 328.

4. *Summarium,* fol. 218.

5. G. M. Gibson, *The Theater of Devotion* (Chicago: University of Chicago Press, 1989); J. C. Coldewey, "The Digby Plays and the Chelmsford Records," *RORD* 18 (1975): 103–21; A. H. Nelson, *Cambridge*, REED (Toronto: University of Toronto Press, 1989).

6. Recent work suggests that there was a Corpus Christi cycle in Doncaster during the sixteenth century; see B. D. Palmer, "Corpus Christi 'Cycles' in Yorkshire: The Surviving Records," *Comparative Drama* 27 (1993): 222–25.

7. A. G. Dickens, *Lollards and Protestants in the Diocese of York, 1509–1558* (London: Hambledon Press, 1982), 141–43.

8. Public Record Office *MS 1/111*, fols. 183–87.

9. British Library *MS Cotton Cleopatra E IV*.

10. *Votaries*, II, 83; *Catalogus*, 171.

11. The plays are cited from my edition: Peter Happé, *The Complete Plays of John Bale*, 2 vols, (Cambridge: Boydell and Brewer, 1985–86).

12. J. S. Brewer and others, eds., *Letters and Papers, Foreign and Domestic, of the Reign of Henry VIII,* 21 vols. (London: HMSO, 1862–1932), XIV.ii, 337; hereafter cited as *L&P.* G. Walker suggests that the A Text of *King Johan* may have been written out for this performance: *Plays of Persuasion* (Cambridge: Cambridge University Press, 1991), 173, n. 12.

13. References to these payments in R. Beadle, "Plays and Playing at Thetford and Nearby," *Theatre Notebook* 32 (1978): 4–11; Nelson, I, 114–15, 119. P. Whitfield White has presented some possible itineraries in *Theatre and Reformation* (Cambridge: Cambridge University Press, 1993), 15–27.

14.   John Foxe, *The Acts and Monuments of John Foxe*, ed. S. R. Cattley and
G. Townsend, 8 vols. (London: Seeley and Burnside, 1837–41), V, 403; hereafter cited as *A&M*.
15.   Walker, 196–205.
16.   B. B. Adams, ed., *John Bale's "King Johan"* (San Marino: The Huntington Library, 1969), 65.
17.   S. Brigden, *London and the Reformation* (Oxford: Oxford University
Press, 1989), 183.
18.   *Image*, 260.
19.   Harris, 29, suggests that this last tract is a defense of Cromwell in a
controversy between Thomas Smith and William Gray in 1540.
20   *L&P* XVII, 177.
21.   *L&P* XXI.i, 611.
22.   See *A&M* V, 565–68, and Harris, 34, for the titles.
23.   Bodley *MS Selden Supra 64*, ed. R. L. Poole and M. Bateson as *Index
Britanniae Scriptorum* (Oxford: Oxford University Press, 1902); revised edition,
ed. C. Brett and J. P. Carley (Cambridge: Boydell and Brewer, 1990); hereafter
cited as *Index*.
24.   Fairfield, 1976, 70.
25.   *A&M* VI, 30–2, 39; Harris, 35.
26.   W. M. H. Hummelen, *Repertorium van het Rederijkersdrama 1500–
ca.1620* (Assen: Van Gorcum, 1968).
27.   *L&P* XX.i, 746.
28.   *A&M* III, 705.
29.   For accounts of the irregular rate of change in religious orientation,
and for many individual variations and changes of direction, see Brigden, *passim*,
and Eamon Duffy, *The Stripping of the Altars* (New Haven: Yale University
Press, 1992), 376–593.
30.   For links with Bale's work see M. Aston, "Lollardry and the
Reformation: Survival or Revival?" *History* xlix (1964):167–70.
31.   Miles Hogarde and James Cancellar both wrote attacks vilifying
Bale's work: see *The Vocacyon of Johan Bale,* ed. Peter Happé & John N. King
(Binghampton: Medieval and Renaissance Texts and Studies, 1990), 16–17;
hereafter cited as *Vocacyon*.
32.   Possibly Singleton was working with John Day, who printed the 10
"Michael Wood" pamphlets in some of which Bale may have had a hand; see
L. P. Fairfield, "The Mysterious Press of 'Michael Wood,'" *The Library*, 5th
series, 27 (1972): 220–32.
33.   *A&M* VIII, 1122.
34.   Christina H. Garrett, *The Marian Exiles* (Cambridge: Cambridge
University Press, 1938), 56; W. Whittingham, *A Brieff Discourse off the Troubles
begonne at Franckford Anno Domini 1554* (Heidelberg: M. Shirat, 1574), ed.
E. Arber (London: privately printed, 1908).
35.   *A&M* VII, 127–28.

36.   Fairfield, 1976, 103.

37.   For Sir Henry Sidney's alleged possession, see M. McKisack, *Medieval History in the Tudor Age* (Oxford: Oxford University Press, 1971), 19. A recent study by William O'Sullivan (see *Selected Bibliography*) has identified new locations for a number of manuscripts.

38.   N. L. Jones, "Matthew Parker, John Bale, and the Magdeburg Centuriators," *Sixteenth Century Journal* 12 (1981): 35–49.

39.   John Strype, *The Life and Acts of Matthew Parker* (London: J. Wyat, 1711), 74; Lambeth Palace MS, dated 6 July 1561.

40.   Fairfield, 1976, 146.

Chapter Two

1.   Brigden, 183.

2.   For the Great Bible and Cromwell's promotion of it, see A. G. Dickens, *The English Reformation,* 2nd ed. (London: B. T. Batsford, 1989), 154–60.

3.   Between 1530 and 1547 at least nine Wycliffite tracts appeared in print in support of the Reformation; see Dickens 1989, 60.

4.   T. R. Trappert, ed., *Selected Writings of Martin Luther*, 4 vols., (Philadelphia: Fortress Press, 1967), II, 38.

5.   Cf. the lost play *In verbi perversores*, *Summarium*, fol. 244, and, with the same incipit, *Contra adulterantes Dei Verbum, Catalogus*, 704.

6.   W. Tyndale, *An Answere to Sir Thomas Mores Dialoge* (Antwerp: S. Cock, 1531), lix.

7.   "Peregrinatio religionis erga," trans. C. R. Thompson, *The Colloquies of Erasmus* (Chicago: University of Chicago Press, 1965), 285–312. The first known English translation appeared in 1536 or 1537 as "The Pilgrimage of Pure Devotion."

8.   "Ther can be none accorde, wher every one wil be a lord," *De Vera Obedientia*, sig. a3ᵛ.

9.   Fairfield, 1976, 57–58. For a parallel, see Thora Balslev Blatt, *The Plays of John Bale* (Copenhagen: G. E. C. Gad, 1968), 68.

10.   Tyndale became increasingly preoccupied with an emphasis upon the law of God after 1530, Dickens 1989, 97.

11.   M. T. Rozett, *The Doctrine of Election and the Emergence of Elizabethan Tragic Practice* (Princeton: Princeton University Press, 1984), 100–102.

12.   Ll.1861–64; cf. ll.1868–74, 1914–18.

13.   Cf. "They can make every daye newe goddes of their lyttle whyte cakes," *Vocacyon*, 62.

14.   On the other hand, Bale translated *The Examination of William Thorpe* into Latin, perhaps with an eye to an international readership.

15.   Foxe tells how Bale's *Oldcastle* persuaded Edward Hall, the chronicler, to change his account of the Lollard; *A&M* III, 377–78.

16. *First Anne Askew*, 1st sig.v; *Latter Anne Askew*, sig. B3: Foxe supports this, *A&M* VI, p. 57.

17. *A&M* V, pp. 537–50.

18. John N. King, *English Reformation Literature* (Princeton: Princeton University Press, 1982), 112.

19. Sig. B1ᵛ: a reference to the alleged false playing of the papists.

20. Christina Garrett, "The Resurrection of the Masse, by Hugh Hilarie—or John Bale?" *The Library*, Fourth Series, xxi (1941): 158.

21. Brigden, 400.

22. On justification by faith, see Dickens 1989, 84.

23. *Votaries* O4ᵛ–O5; King, 198–9.

24. The conflict between the persecuted Protestant Church and the cruel papists is epitomized on the title page of *Vocation.* See figure 3 and the Note on the Illustrations.

25. St. Augustine, *The City of God* (Harmondsworth: Penguin Books, 1984), book XI, chapter 1; in this section Augustine deals with the origin of the two cities.

26. Bale may have been influenced by the Lutheran Joachim van Watt (pseud. Judas Nazarei), whose *Vom Alteren und neuen Gott, Glauben und Lehre* (Basel: A. Petri, 1521) was translated by William Turner as *A worke entytled of the olde god and the newe* (London: W. Marshall, 1534). Bale apparently knew this work and disapproved of it before his conversion; Fairfield, 1976, 70, and notes 45 and 46.

27. Honor C. McCusker, *John Bale: Dramatist and Antiquary* (Bryn Mawr, 1942), 61.

28. 1503; the English translation published in 1533 may or may not have been by Tyndale. See A. M. O'Donnell, ed., *Erasmus: Enchiridion Militis Christi*, EETS 282 (Oxford: Oxford University Press, 1981), xlix–liii.

29. L. P. Fairfield, 1971, 331; 1972, 220.

Chapter Three

1. See W. T. Davies, "A Bibliography of John Bale," *Oxford Bibliographical Society, Proceedings and Papers* 5 (1940): 203–79 (244–46); and G. Mentz, *Handschriften der Reformationzeit* (Bonn: A. Marcus and E. Weber, 1912), 5.

2. The best accounts of the manuscripts are in McCusker, 97–111, and Fairfield, 1976, 157–71.

3. See chapter 1, note 23.

4. Public Record Office MS, *SP 1/111*, fols. 183–87.

5. The manuscript is described by McCusker, 97–98; Fairfield (1976, 159) notes that the latest item is dated 20 January 1528.

6. Fol. 112ᵛ, illustrated in Harris, 134. This shows that Bale added the incipit for *King Johan*, which, as it happens, does not accord with the first line of the extant manuscript: see this volume, p. 90, and Adams, 21–22.

7. J. Crompton, "Fasciculi Zizaniorum," *Journal of Ecclesiastical History* 12 (1961): 40.
8. *De Viris Illustribus* (Augsburg: Günther Zanier, 1472).
9. British Library *MS Harley 3838*, fols. 118–55; see Harris, 111.
10. McCusker, 38, nos. 84–92, presumably all manuscripts.
11. *A&M* III, 705.
12. Extant as Trinity College, Cambridge, *MS R.7.15*.
13. Fol. 2ᵛ. Fairfield, 1976, 209, n.116.
14. Bale extends his praise in the *Summarium: Antiquitatis Britannicae fervidus amator ac diligentissimus inquisitor* ("Fervent lover of British antiquity and most diligent enquirer," fol. 240).
15. The *Summarium* has five centuries and some notes for a sixth; *Catalogus* appeared in two parts with nine centuries in the first and five in the second, and with an index for each part. Bale's own biography ends the eighth century.

Chapter Four

1. Harris, 2.
2. For other references to matters devilish, see ll. 378 ("polycye"), 383, 392 (conjuring), 404, 416, 619, 755, 762, 1087, 1134, and 1545.
3. "In Anglica regione primus habebatur, post Ioannem Vuicleuum," *Catalogus*, 658.
4. The fact that one of the other surviving plays concerns God's promises is perhaps no accident, for the law and the promises were seen as complementary.
5. Blatt, 182. There is a strong defense of Bale's reputation as a stylist, with emphasis upon his Latin rather than his English, in King, 57–61.
6. Since the use of a comma in modern style would be distracting, I have here followed the convention of showing caesura by a brief gap in each line.
7. Bede, *Homilia XCV De Nativitate Domini* in J. P. Migne, *Patrologiae Cursus Completus {Patrologia Latina}* (Paris: 1842–40), 94, col. 498 (cited as *PL* hereafter): my translation. Bale lists more than eighty manuscripts of Bede's work in the *Index*, 40–46.
8. *PL* 202, col. 33.
9. E. H. Weatherly, ed., *Speculum Sacerdotale*, EETS o.s. 200 (Oxford: Oxford University Press, 1936), 7.
10. William Tyndale, *The Obedience of a Christen Man and how Christen Rulers Ought to Governe* (Antwerp: J. Hoochstraten, 1528), sigs. Lii–Liii.
11. *Exposition*; quoted by Craik, 74. The passage by St Paul is actually concerned to show that Moses himself put on the veil to conceal the bright light in his countenance, which the Jews could not look upon.

Chapter Five

1. J .P. Collier, ed., *Kynge Johan: A Play in Two Parts by John Bale* (London: Camden Society, 1838). The account of the text given here is based

upon the subsequent editions by J. H. P. Pafford (1931), and Barry B. Adams (1969). See the Selected Bibliography.

    2.   Pafford, xvii–xviii.

    3.   Compare ll. 2680–81 with ll. 2626–31.

    4.   Line 1112, in the Interpretour's speech, which was added to the A text by Bale.

    5.   Davies, 244–46.

    6.   Ll. 1378–80, 1694, 1809–70, 1914–40; for details, see Peter Happé, "Sedition in Kyng Johan: Bale's Development of a Vice," *Medieval English Theatre* 3 (1981): 3–6.

    7.   Simon Fish, *A Supplicacyon for the Beggers* (Antwerp: J. Grapheus, 1529), 3^{r-v}; R. Barnes, *A Supplicacion unto the most gracyous prynce H. the viii* (London: J. Byddell, 1534), fols. $B4^v$–B6. Bale has Veritas assert that many chroniclers had praised Johan (ll. 2193–206), with the exception of Polydore Vergil, whom Bale saw as a distorting papist. However, Adams has shown that Bale drastically improved Johan's reputation as presented by these writers (25–30).

    8.   See E. S. Miller, "The Roman Rite in Bale's *King Johan*," *PMLA* LXIV (1949): 802–22.

    9.   For example, Crafty Conveyaunce becomes Good Demeynaunce at ll. 669–75.

    10.   ll. 2347–48, 2358–59, and see the whole speech, ll. 2346–60.

    11.   There are more proverbs in this play than in the others; see the list in Blatt, 213–14.

    12.   Background information here is taken from J. J. Scarisbrick, *Henry VIII* (London: Methuen, 1976) and Christopher Haigh, *English Reformations*, (Oxford: Oxford University Press, 1993). For some particular applications, I am indebted to Walker, 169–221.

    13.   Scarisbrick, 468.

    14.   Scarisbrick, 478.

    15.   In 1539 a player called Spenser, an ex-priest, was burned at Salisbury for ridiculing the Sacrament. V. C. Gildersleeve, *Government Regulation of the Elizabethan Drama* (New York: Columbia Univesity Press, 1908), 21.

    16.   Haigh, 152.

    17.   J. E. Cox, ed., *Miscellaneous Writings and Letters of Thomas Cranmer*, Parker Society (Cambridge: Cambridge University Press, 1846), 388.

Chapter Six

    1.   Ruth Blackburn points out that there is a very close parallel to Bale's selection of characters in the *Speculum Naturale* of Vincent of Beauvais; see her *Biblical Drama under the Tudors* (The Hague: Mouton, 1971), 54 and n. 51.

    2.   I have explored Bale's interpretation in Peter Happé "*The Temptation of Our Lord*: Bale's Adaptation of the Scriptural Narrative" (forthcoming).

3.   For details of this theory, see Timothy Fry, "The Unity of the *Ludus Coventriae*," *Studies in Philology* 48 (1951): 527–70.

4.   Compare ll. 355–79 with Genesis 18:23–32; see Blatt, 94.

5.   The view presented here follows the chronology suggested by the dates in *Anglorum Heliades* and *Summarium*. We must leave open, however, the possibility that this assumption is incorrect and that the biblical plays may have preceded the other two. We might then suppose that the biblical plays represented an earlier phase in Bale's development as a dramatist, but even if this were so, the complementary view advanced here that they were written with different dramatic intentions can still be sustained from the evidence adduced.

Chapter Seven

1.   For details of the extent of Heywood's activities as an entertainer, see Richard Axton and Peter Happé (eds.), *The Plays of John Heywood* (Cambridge: Boydell and Brewer), 3–9.

2.   Proposals for doubling schemes for the five plays are set out in Peter Happé *Complete Plays* I, 152–56.

3.   Ll. 700–02; "Grant, we beg, that just as we live by their (the laity's) sweat, so we may deserve to enjoy perpetually their wives, daughters, and maidservants."

4.   "Properties and Costumes in the Plays of John Bale," *Medieval English Theatre* 2 (1980): 55–65.

5.   There is a comparable precedent in the fifteenth-century morality play *Wisdom*: "entreth Lucyfer in a dewyllys (devil's) aray wythowt and wythin as a prowde galonte," stage direction before l. 325 in M. Eccles (ed.), *The Macro Plays,* EETS 262 (Oxford: Oxford University Press, 1969), 125.

Chapter Eight

1.   "*Biliosus Baleus* passeth for his true character," *Worthies of England* (London: I.G.W.L. and W.G. , 1662), 61.

2.   See King, 373. This work contains an excellent account of Bale's influence, and I acknowledge here, with pleasure, a considerable debt to it.

3.   King, 429. See also King's account (324–26) of how Bale's initial attribution of *Piers Plowman* to Wyclif and his historical scheme in *Image* may have influenced Robert Crowley in his edition of *The Vision of Pierce Plowman* in 1550.

4.   For further notices of Bale's work in the seventeenth and eighteenth centuries, including that by Fuller in *Abel Redidivus* (London, J. Stafford, 1651), see Harris, 10.

5.   See Axton and Happé, 6–7.

6.   *Wether* was probably printed late in 1533, and *Love* probably early in 1534.

7. Alternating structure is discussed by David M. Bevington, in *From "Mankind" to Marlowe* (Cambridge, Mass.: Harvard University Press, 1962), 152–69.

8. Ll. 412 to 440: references to the edition by J. M. Nosworthy, for the Malone Society (Oxford: Oxford University Press, 1971).

9. References are to the edition by Frederick Ives Carpenter (Chicago: University of Chicago Press, 1902).

10. References to *New Custom* are from the Tudor Facsimile Text, ed. J. S. Farmer (London: T. C. Jack and E. C. Jack, 1908); for *Enough*, see the (modernized) edition by R. Mark Benbow (London: Edward Arnold, 1968).

11. Sig. A4^r; quoted by White, 91 and 95, who identifies this play with William Wager's *Enough is as Good as a Feast, the Trial of Treasure*, and with Thomas Lupton's *All for Money*, as Protestant plays particularly concerned with the themes of money, and especially usury.

12. See Willard Farnham, *The Medieval Heritage of Elizabethan Tragedy* (Berkeley and Los Angeles: University of California Press, 1936; reprinted Oxford: Oxford University Press, 1963).

Selected Bibliography

PRIMARY SOURCES

Published Works

Plays

A Tragedye or Enterlude manyfestyng the Chefe Promyses of God unto Man by All Ages in the Olde Lawe, from the Fall of Adam to the Incarnacyon of the Lorde Jesus Christ (God's Promises). Compyled by Johan Bale, Anno Domini M.D.XXXVIII. Wesel: Dirk van der Straten, ?1547.

A Brefe Comedy or Enterlude of Johan Baptystes Preachynge in the Wyldernesse, openynge the Craftye Assaultes of the Hypocrytes, with the Gloryouse Baptyme of the Lorde Jesus Christ (John Baptist's Preaching). Compyled by Johan Bale, Anno Domini M.D.XXXVIII. ?Wesel: Dirk van der Straten, 1547. In *The Harleian Miscellany*. London: T. Osborne, 1744.

A Brefe Comedy or Enterlude concernynge The Temptacyon of our Lorde and Saver Jesus Christ by Sathan in the Desart (The Temptation). Compyled by Johan Bale, Anno Domini M.D.XXXVIII. Wesel: Dirk van der Straten, ?1547.

A Comedy concernynge Thre Lawes of Nature, Moses and Christ, corrupted by the Sodomytes, Pharysees and Papystes (Three Laws). Compyled by Johan Bale, Anno Domini M.D.XXXVIII. Wesel: Dirk van der Straten, ?1548.

King Johan by John Bale. Edited by J. H. Pafford and W. W. Greg, for the Malone Society. Oxford: Oxford University Press, 1931.

John Bale's "King Johan." Edited by B. B. Adams. San Marino: The Huntington Library, 1969.

The Complete Plays of John Bale. Edited by Peter Happé. 2 vols. Cambridge: Boydell and Brewer, 1985–86.

Other Writings

Bibliographies

Illustrium maioris Britannie Scriptorium . . . Summarium. Wesel: Dirk van der Straten, 1548.

Scriptorum Illustrium maioris Britanniae . . . Catalogus. 2 vols. Basel: J. Oporinus, 1557–59.

Polemical Works

NOTE: These works are arranged alphabetically by the short titles cited in this book.

Acta Romanorum Pontificum
     Acta Romanorum Pontificum. Basel: J. Oporinus, 1558.
Answer . . . Papistical Exhortation
     An answere to a papystycall exhortacyon. Antwerp: S. Mierdman, 1548.
Apology
     The Apology of Johan Bale agaynste a ranke Papyst. London: J. Day, 1550.
Baptista Mantuanus
     A lamentable complaynte of Baptista Mantuanus. London: J. Day, 1551.
Customable Swearers
     A Christen Exhortacyon unto Customable Swearers. Antwerp: widow of C. Ruremond, 1543.
De Vera Obedientia
     De Vera Obediencia. London: ?J. Day, 1553.
Declaration
     A Declaration of Edmonde Bonners articles. London: F. Coldocke, 1561.
Dialogue
     A dialogue or Communycacyon to be had at table betwene two chyldren. London: R. Foster, 1549.
Epistle Exhortatory
     The epistle exhortatorye of an Englyshe Chrystyane. Antwerp: widow of C. Ruremond, 1544.
First Anne Askew
     The first examinacyon of Anne Askewe. Wesel: Dirk van der Straten, 1546.
Frantic Papist
     An Expostulation or complaynte agaynste the blasphemyes of a franticke papyst of Hamshyre. London: J. Day, 1552.
Godly Meditation
     A Godly Medytacyon of the christen sowle . . . compyled in frenche by lady Margarete quene of Naverre . . . translated into Englysh by the ryght vertuouse lady Elyzabeth. Wesel: Dirk van der Straten, 1548.
Image
     The Image of bothe churches. Antwerp: S. Mierdman, 1545.
John Lambert
     A Treatyse made by Johan Lambert. Wesel: Dirk van der Straten, 1548.
John Pomerane
     A Compendious letter which Ihon Pomerane sent to Englande. Southwark: J. Nicholson, 1536.
Laborious Journey
     The laboryouse Journey & serche of Johan Lelande. London: J. Bale, 1549.

Latter Anne Askew
    The lattre examinacyon of Anne Askewe. Wesel: Dirk van der Straten, 1547.
Man of Sin
    A dysclosynge or openynge of the Manne of synne. Antwerp: A. Goinus, 1543.
Martin Luther
    The true hystorie of the Christen departynge of the reverende man, D. Martyne Luther. Wesel: Dirk van der Straten, 1546.
Mystery of Iniquity
    A Mysterye of inyquyty. Antwerp: A. Goinus, 1545.
Oldcastle
    A brefe Chronycle concernynge the Examinacyon and death of the blessed martyr of Christ syr Johan Oldecastell. Antwerp: A. Goinus, 1544.
Pageant of Popes
    The Pageant of Popes. London: T. Marshe, 1574.
Resurrection
    The Resurrection of the Masse. ?Wesel: J. Lambrecht, 1554.
Rhithmi
    Rhithmi Vetustissimi de Corrupto Ecclesiae Statu. Wesel: Dirk van der Straten, 1546.
Romish Fox
    Yet a course at the Romyshe Foxe. Antwerp: A. Goinus, 1543.
Two Neighbours
    A Dialogue or Familiar talke betwene two neighbours. London: ?J. Day, 1554.
Vocation
    The vocacyon of Johan Bale to the bishoprick of Ossorie in Irelande. Wesel: J. Lambrecht for Hugh Singleton, 1553. Edited by Peter Happé and John N. King. Binghampton: Medieval and Renaissance Texts and Studies, 1990.
Votaries
    The Actes of Englysh votaryes. Antwerp: S. Mierdman, 1546.

Manuscripts

NOTE: Most of the manuscripts are complex collections arbitrarily bound together; for fuller details, see Fairfield, 1976, 157–64.

Bodleian Library *MS. Selden Supra 41*. Contains *Fasciculus Carmelitarum*, a history of the Carmelites up to 1540, including the Reformation; lives of Carmelite saints; and selections from Carmelite authors, including Baptista Mantuanus.

Bodleian Library *MS. Selden Supra 64*. Edited by R. L. Poole and Mary Bateson as *Index Britanniae Scriptorum*. Oxford: Oxford University Press, 1902. Second edition by C. Brett and J. P. Carley. Cambridge: Boydell and Brewer, 1990. A list of English authors with indispensable information about places where Bale saw manuscripts.

British Library *MS. Harley 1819*. Identified as the *Collectiones Gallicas*, being notes that Bale made in France c. 1527. It contains religious poems, some by Bale, and a life of St. Anne.

British Library *MS. Harley 3838*. Contains *Anglorum Heliades*; *Scriptores ab Helie*, a mythical history of the Carmelites; and *Scriptores a Bertoldo*, a history of the order from 1100 to the 1530s.

Huntington Library *MS. HM3*. King Johan.

Public Record Office *MS. SP 1/111*, (fols. 183–87). *Answer to certain Articles. The Answer of John Bale pryst unto serten articles unjustlye gadred upon hys prechyng.* ?January 1537.

Trinity College, Cambridge *MS. R.7.15*. Bale's transcript of John Leland's *De Viris Illustribus*, after 1552.

Works by Others

Erasmus, Desiderius. *The Colloquies of Erasmus*. Translated by C. R. Thompson. Chicago: University of Chicago Press, 1965.

————. *Erasmus: Enchiridion Militis Christi*. Edited by A. M. O'Donnell. EETS 282. Oxford: Oxford University Press, 1981.

Fish, Simon. *A Supplicacyon for the Beggers*. ?Antwerp: J. Grapheus, 1529.

Foxe, John. *The Acts and Monuments of John Foxe*. Edited by S. R. Cattley and G. Townsend. 8 vols. London: Seeley and Burnside, 1837–41.

Heywood, John. *The Plays of John Heywood*. Edited by Richard Axton and Peter Happé. Cambridge: Boydell and Brewer, 1991.

Luther, Martin. *Selected Writings of Martin Luther*. Edited by T. R. Trappert. 4 vols. Philadelphia: Fortress Press, 1967.

Macro Plays. Edited by M. Eccles. EETS 262. Oxford: Oxford University Press, 1969.

New Custom. Edited by J. S. Farmer. Tudor Facsimile Text. London and Edinburgh: T. C. Jack and E. C. Jack, 1908.

Tyndale, William. *The Obedience of a Christen Man and how Christen rulers ought to governe*. Antwerp: J. Hoochstraten, 1528.

————. *An Answere to Sir Thomas Mores Dialoge*. Antwerp: S. Cock, 1531.

Wager, Lewis. *The Life and Repentance of Mary Magdalene*. Edited by Frederick Ives Carpenter. Chicago: University of Chicago Press, 1902.

Wager, William. *Enough is as Good as a Feast*. Edited by R. Mark Benbow. London: Edward Arnold, 1968.

Wever, Richard. *An Interlude of Lusty Juventus*. Edited by J. M. Nosworthy, for the Malone Society. Oxford: Oxford University Press, 1971.

SECONDARY SOURCES

Bibliographies

Davies, William T. "A Bibliography of John Bale." *Oxford Bibliographical Society Proceedings and Papers* 5 (1940): 203–79. Valuable for comprehensive and coherent biography, and for detailed lists of printed and manuscript works.

Happé, Peter. "Recent Studies in John Bale." *English Literary Renaissance* 17 (1987): 103–13. Reviews and assesses scholarship and editions up to 1987.

STC. *A Short-Title Catalogue of Books Printed in England, Scotland and Ireland, and of English Books Printed Abroad, 1475–1640*. Edited by W. A. Jackson, F. J. Ferguson, and K. F. Panzer. 2 vols. London: The Bibliographical Society, 1976 and 1986.

Books

Aston, M. *England's Iconoclasts*. Oxford: Oxford University Press, 1988. A wide-ranging account of the destruction of iconography, in which Bale's special defense of Edward VI as a young Josiah is noted.

Bevington, David M. *From "Mankind" to Marlowe*. Cambridge, Mass.: Harvard University Press, 1962. Starting from the morality plays, traces the development of troupe disciplines in the interludes with particular reference to the effect upon structure.

————. *Tudor Drama and Politics: A Critical Approach to Topical Meaning*. Cambridge, Mass.: Harvard University Press, 1968. Identifies Bale as a leader of the Protestant cause in his advocacy of the need to persuade King Henry by the parallel with King Johan as one defying the papacy.

Blackburn, Ruth H. *Biblical Drama under the Tudors*. The Hague: Mouton, 1971. Surveys the variety of biblical drama outside the Corpus Christi plays. The section on Bale deals with some important aspects of his medieval roots, together with the impact of Lutheran theology.

Blatt, Thora Balslev. *The Plays of John Bale*. Copenhagen: G. E. C. Gad, 1968. One of the few studies devoted exclusively to the plays, this work gives much important information about their background and evolution, including attention to late medieval theology.

Brigden, Susan. *London and the Reformation*. Oxford: Oxford University Press, 1989. Pays close attention to late medieval Catholicism and the transition to Protestantism which dominated life in London for most of the sixteenth century. Helps to place the work of dramatists in a wider religious context.

Craik, T. W. *The Tudor Interlude*. Leicester: Leicester University Press, 1958. A pioneering study of the staging of the interludes with excellent details of stage, costume and dress. One of the few books to be aware of the positive stage qualities of this dramatic form. Pays attention to *King Johan* and *Three Laws*.

Dickens, A. G. *Lollards and Protestants in the Diocese of York*. London: Hambledon Press, 1959. Makes a close study of a region in which Bale worked for a time. The author discusses especially individual lives at a time of marked religious change.

———. *The English Reformation*. London: B. T. Batsford, 2d edition, 1989. First published in 1964, this remains the standard work on the subject, invaluable for details of many leading Protestant figures. The author addresses the important question of the relationship between Lollardry and Protestantism.

Duffy, Eamon. *The Stripping of the Altars*. New Haven: Yale University Press, 1992. A monumental and highly readable accumulation of written and visual information about the religion of pre-Reformation England written from a Catholic viewpoint. Makes a special study of religious change in the light of the twists in official policies, and contains some very interesting information about the provinces.

Fairfield, Leslie P. *John Bale: Mythmaker for the English Reformation*. West Lafayette: Purdue University Press, 1976. A detailed study of Bale's life, his polemical writings, and the development of his views of Protestant history and myth. Contains an excellent bibliography of the printed works, and catalogs the contents of the composite manuscripts.

Firth, Katherine R. *The Apocalyptic Tradition in Reformation Britain, 1530–1645*. Oxford: Oxford University Press, 1979. Studies Bale's adaptation and development of interpretations of Revelations as seen in the prose works, chiefly *Image*. Especially useful on influence of Wyclif and on Bale's use of imagery and of the structure implied in the biblical narrative.

Fox, Alistair. *Politics and Literature in the Reigns of Henry VII and Henry VIII*. Oxford: Basil Blackwell, 1989. This extensive account of the subject gives a useful account of King Johan as a character embodying Bale's perception of Henry VIII, which points up Henry's interest in subduing the clergy and asserting sovereignty. Somewhat marred by the author's low opinion of Bale as a dramatist.

Garrett, Christina Hallowell. *The Marian Exiles: A Study in the Origins of Elizabethan Puritanism*. Cambridge: Cambridge University Press, 1938. Contains first-hand research on Bale's exiles and gives valuable information about his movements on the Continent during a time of strife.

Gibson, G. M. *The Theater of Devotion*. Chicago: University of Chicago Press, 1989. A well-resourced study of the religious life of East Anglia, with special attention to the possible theatrical nexus around Bury St. Edmunds. Gives close attention to iconography and worship before the Reformation.

Haigh, Christopher. *English Reformations*. Oxford: Oxford University Press, 1993. This historical examination of the period questions official policy and attends to the important contemporary interest in the unneven nature of the Reformation, especially in terms of popular belief.

Harris, Jesse W. *John Bale*. Urbana: Illinois Studies in Language and Literature 25, 1940. A chronological account of Bale's life, full of useful and rarely noted information. Pays special attention to the pamphlets and controversial works, including the manuscripts, using them to strengthen the biography.

Hummelen, W. M. H. *Repertorium van het Rederijkersdrama 1500–ca.1620*. Assen: Van Gorcum, 1968. A collection of information, including details of title pages, brings together in one list the very large number of Dutch plays written for the Rhetoricians' Chambers. This would be the theatrical context into which Bale entered during his exile in the Netherlands.

Kendall, Ritchie D. *The Drama of Dissent: The Radical Poetics of Nonconformity, 1380–1590*. Chapel Hill: University of North Carolina Press, 1986. Considers the work of a number of writers in different genres whose work lies outside established religion: attempts to show dramatic aspects of most of them and to develop an awareness of the religious context of protest, including especially *Three Laws*.

King, John N. *English Reformation Literature*. Princeton: Princeton University Press, 1982. A radical reappraisal of its subject; rescues many Protestant writers from oblivion and develops an account of a significant literary tradition throughout the sixteenth century. Includes an important bibliography of Protestant writings.

Levy, F. J. *Tudor Historical Thought*. San Marino: The Huntington Library, 1967. Notices and elaborates upon the continuity of Bale scholarship from Bale's Carmelite days to his last work on the *Catalogus*. Discusses the importance of Bale's popularization of history.

McConica, J. K. *English Humanists and Reformation Politics*. Oxford: Oxford University Press, 1965. An exceptionally learned and well-balanced survey of humanism in the sixteenth century which follows the influence of Erasmus and his disciples; touches Bale in respect to *King Johan* and *Anne Askew*.

McCusker, Honor C. *John Bale: Dramatist and Antiquary*. Bryn Mawr, 1942. A rich and well-informed study of Bale's works, strong on the bibliographical context, including Bale's printers; identifies Dirk van der Straten, the chief of them. Discusses the important aspects of Bale's sources and his collection of books and manuscripts.

McKisack, Mary. *Medieval History in the Tudor Age*. Oxford: The Clarendon Press, 1971. Examines Bale's work as a bibliographer and discusses the importance of his link with John Leland.

Nelson, Alan H. *Cambridge*, REED. Toronto: University of Toronto Press, 1989. A comprehensive approach to stage, secular music, and civic entertain-

ment in Cambridge; relevant for the context in which Bale spent most of
his early years as undergraduate and graduate.

Phillips, John. *The Reformation of Images: Destruction of Art in England, 1535–1664*.
Berkeley and Los Angeles: University of California Press, 1973. A rich
account of the development of iconoclasm in England over more than a
century; provides many useful details from particular localities.

Roston, Murray. *Biblical Drama in England from the Middle Ages to the Present
Day*. London: Faber and Faber, 1968. Concentrates in dealing with Bale
upon the possible influence of Luther, and upon links with Calvin.

Scarisbrick, J. J. *Henry VIII*. London: Methuen, 1976. An indispensable account
of the life of King Henry, with close attention to his participation in
international affairs. Includes much valuable information on Cromwell.

Sperk, Klaus. *Mittelalterliche Tradition und reformatorische Polemik in den Spielen
John Bales*. Heidelberg: Carl Winter, 1973. Considers the contrast
between medieval dramatic tradition and the development of Protestant
ideology. Places Bale's plays in relation to East Anglian drama of the late
Middle Ages.

Spivack, Bernard. *Shakespeare and the Allegory of Evil*. New York: Columbia
University Press, 1958. The most comprehensive study of the Vice to be
published in recent years; pays a great deal of attention to the Vice in
interludes, with Infidelity in *Three Laws* as a significant example.

Walker, G. *Plays of Persuasion*. Cambridge: Cambridge University Press, 1991.
Contains careful and effective discussion of the political context of *King
Johan*, along with studies of the circumstances surrounding the writing
and performance of plays by other authors.

Weimann, Robert. *Shakespeare and the Popular Tradition in the Theater*. Edited by
Robert Schwarz. Baltimore: The John Hopkins Press, 1987. In studying
many aspects of theatrical activity, pays special attention to Sedition in
King Johan in terms of wordplay and subversive language.

White, Paul Whitfield. *Theatre and Reformation*. Cambridge: Cambridge
University Press, 1993. Discusses in depth two important aspects of Bale
studies: some of the possible circumstances of performance including the
organization of Bale's acting troupe, and the place of the plays in relation
to other Protestant interludes.

Articles and Essays

Aston, M. "Lollardry and the Reformation: Survival or Revival?" *History* xlix
(1964):149–70. Discusses the provenance of some Protestant ideas with
particular reference to Lollardry; valuable for a consideration of the use of
manuscript sources by Bale and Foxe in treating Sir John Oldcastle.

———. "John Wycliffe's Reformation Reputation." *Past and Present* 30 (1965):
24–26. Assesses the contribution made by Bale to Wyclif's reputation,
with special consideration of the *Summarium*.

Carpenter, Sarah. "John Bale's *Kynge Johan*: The Dramatisation of Allegorical and Non-Allegorical Figures." In *Le Théâtre au Moyen Age*, edited by Gary R. Muller. Quebec: Les Editions Univers (1981): 263–69. Addresses the important question of the characteristics of allegorical figures and their relationship to personalized human beings on stage.

Crompton, J. "Fasciculi Zizaniorum." *Journal of Ecclesiastical History* 12 (1961): 35–45, 155–66. Valuable account of this important manuscript collection of Wycliffite documents, part of Bodleian *MS e Musaeo 86*: traces its provenance, and discusses Bale's acquisition of the collection and the use he made of it.

Fairfield, L. P. "The *Vocacyon of Johan Bale* and Early English Autobiography." *Renaissance Quarterly* 24 (1971): 327–40. Considers the place of *Vocacyon* in the development of autobiography, but prefers to see this work as part of the Protestants' interest in creating their own hagiography.

————. "The Mysterious Press of 'Michael Wood.'" *The Library*, 5th series, 27 (1972): 220–32. Discusses the production of 10 pamphlets by the printer John Day under the pseudonym Michael Wood, which Bale had used earlier; two of the pamphlets are attributed to Bale.

Fry, Timothy. "The Unity of the *Ludus Coventriae*." *Studies in Philology* 48 (1951): 527–70. Using evidence from nondramatic theological sources, presents the theory of the abuse of power by Satan in seeking the death of Christ; the so-called *Ludus Coventriae* (now known as the *N. Town Cycle*) is seen as the most coherent example.

Greg, W. W. "Notes on Some Early Plays." *The Library* 11 (1930): 44–56. Shows that the lost sixteenth-century edition of *John Baptist's Preaching*, as reprinted in 1744, was originally printed in sequence with *Temptation*.

Happé, Peter. "Properties and Costumes in the Plays of John Bale." *Medieval English Theatre* 2 (1980): 55–65. Presents the evidence that can be collected from the texts of the plays, including the stage directions, to show Bale's conscious attention to both costumes and properties.

————. "Sedition in *Kyng Johan*: Bale's Development of a Vice." *Medieval English Theatre* 3 (1981): 3–6. Considers the additions to the part of the Vice, to show that Bale increased the theatricality of the part, perhaps in conformity with a developing convention.

————. "The Protestant Adaptation of the Saint Play." In *The Saint Play in Medieval Europe*, edited by Clifford Davidson. Kalamazoo: The Medieval Institute Publications (1986): 205–40. Investigates the process, possibly initiated by Bale, in which an attempt was made to create Protestant figures equivalent to saints. The theme is traced in a number of interludes by other playwrights.

McCusker, Honor C. "Books and MSS formerly in the Possession of John Bale." *The Library*, Fourth Series, 16 (1936): 144–65. Lists the books Bale lost in Ireland in 1553, and traces the later whereabouts of some of them.

Miller, Edwin S. "The Roman Rite in Bale's *King Johan*." *PMLA* LXIV (1949): 802–22. A highly informative account of the liturgical sources for significant musical items performed in *King Johan*: notes the importance of the dramatic effects.

———. "The Antiphons in Bale's Cycle of Christ." *Annali Istituo, Universitario Napoli, Sezione Germanica* 3 (1940): 629–38. Identifies the liturgical place of the antiphons in *God's Promises*, and shows that they are related to Advent.

O'Sullivan, William. "The Irish 'remnaunt' of John Bale's manuscripts." In *New Science Out of Old Books: Studies in Manuscripts and Early Printed Books in Honour of A. I. Doyle*, edited by Richard Beadle and A. J. Piper. Aldershot: Scholar Press, 1995. By tracing Bale's movements and some of his associates in Ireland, the author has succeeded in some further locations of items from Bale's library beyond those already noted by McCusker (above). He usefully questions the accuracy and completeness of Bale's list.

Pineas, Rainer. "The Polemical Drama of John Bale." In *Shakespeare and Dramatic Tradition: Essays in Honor of S. F. Johnson*, edited by W. R. Elton and William B. Long. Newark: University of Delaware Press (1989): 194–210. Studies a variety of rhetorical devices used by Bale, especially self-condemnation and other revelatory techniques by the evil characters. Deeply concerned about Bale's distortion of received information.

———. "John Bale's Non-Dramatic Works of Religious Controversy." *Studies in the Renaissance* 9 (1962): 218–33. An important review of Bale's prose works which brings out relationships between them, and identifies some source material.

———. "William Tyndale's Influence on John Bale's Polemical Use of History." *Archiv für Reformationsgeschichte* 53 (1962): 79–96. Traces the important links between Bale and Tyndale, suggesting a strong dependence by Bale on Tyndale's theology.

Potter, Lois. "John Bale." In *The Revels History of Drama in English: Volume II, 1500–1576*. Edited by Norman Sanders, Richard Southern, T. W. Craik, and Lois Potter. London and New York: Methuen (1980): 177–85. An account of several of Bale's dramatic devices including the sermon, the Vice, and the apocalyptic tradition; also includes consideration of some tragic aspects of *King Johan*.

Steele, R. "Notes on English Books Printed Abroad." *Transactions of the Bibliographical Society* XI (1909–11):189–236. Discusses the "Marburg" type used in the publication of Tyndale's work and connects it with a significant list of Bale's works, including the plays, printed at Wesel.

Unpublished Dissertations and Theses

Bailey, Gabrielle A. "Aspects of Reformation Theology in the Plays of John Bale." University of Waterloo, 1981. Makes a particular study of Tyndale's influence on Bale, and on the development of Tyndale's ideas in *Three Laws* and *King Johan*.

Duncan, R. L. "Protestant Themes and Theses in the Drama of John Bale." Indiana University, 1964. A thorough review of Bale's theological imperatives; brings out his attention to papal immorality, the weakness of scholasticism, the role of the monarch, and the importance of *sola scriptura*.

Index

The Author

Peter Happé is the retired principal of Barton Peveril Sixth Form College in Hampshire, England. He read English at Queens' College, Cambridge, and later went on to do research at Birkbeck College, London University, where he wrote M.A. and Ph.D. theses on Tudor Drama. He has published articles on this field in several journals, including *Comparative Drama, Medieval English Theatre*, and *English Literary Renaissance*. His editions of early plays have included three anthologies for Penguin, and more recently *Two Moral Interludes* for the Malone Society and *The Complete Plays of John Bale*. He co-edited *The Vocacyon of Johan Bale* with John N. King, and *The Plays of John Heywood* with Richard Axton. He has also published an edition of Ben Jonson's *The Devil Is an Ass* in the Revels Plays (Manchester University Press).

In 1994 he was Professeur Associé at the Université François Rabelais in Tours. At present he is teaching for the Open University and for Southampton University, and he is working on a book entitled *English Drama Before Shakespeare*, and on comparative aspects of English, French, and Dutch late medieval drama.